That Tree TALKED to me

Photos & Stories
CATHRYN WELLNER

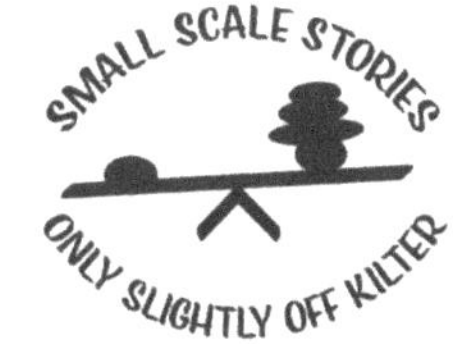

Small Scale Stories #1
Espoir Press
British Columbia 2017

Espoir Press
1002 - 1128 Sunset Drive
Kelowna, British Columbia
Canada V1Y 9W7

©2017 Cathryn Wellner

All rights reserved. Photographs and text are by Cathryn Wellner and may not be reproduced in any format or context, other than in reviews. For any other use, please contact cathryn@cathrynwellner.com.

That Tree Talked to Me (Small Scale Stories #1)

ISBN 978-0-9951653-8-0

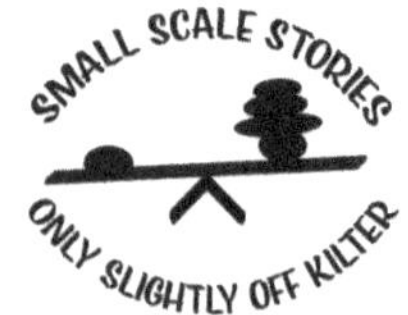

INTRODUCTION

Joni Mitchell nailed it when she wrote, "We are stardust." Scientists have a rational explanation. Exploding galaxies disperse minute bits of matter. The ones that land on our planet eventually form water, mountains, and people.

Parts of our fingers are as old as the universe. Pieces of our intestines may have landed on this planet in the last century. If we had funerals for body cells, we would be grieving every minute of the day. If we celebrated the birth of each new cell, we would be partying non-stop.

After our death, our stardust disperses, recombines, and becomes trees, wolves, soil and carrots. When scientists and spiritual leaders claim everything is interconnected, they are not exaggerating. That tree you climbed is a relative.

As a child, I hugged trees a lot. I talked to stray cats and listened to the stories grass told. I knew in my bones we were one big, challenging family.

What happened was predictable. I grew up, got busy, and forgot we are related to everything we touch.

A few years ago I started carrying a camera on my daily walks. Wherever I pointed the lens, stardust relatives told stories. They insisted I share them.

Instagram and Facebook friends nudged me to put the small tales into books. This is the first. More are on the way.

Your stardust bits will insist on telling different stories when they recognize relatives in the photos. That's what makes this so much fun.

So listen to the tree whose stardust is in the paper of this book (and in the mysterious bits and bytes of the digital version). Your stardust relatives have traveled the galaxies. Hear their stories. Share them. Be inspired. Be inspiring.

We are stardust. We are one, big, complicated family.

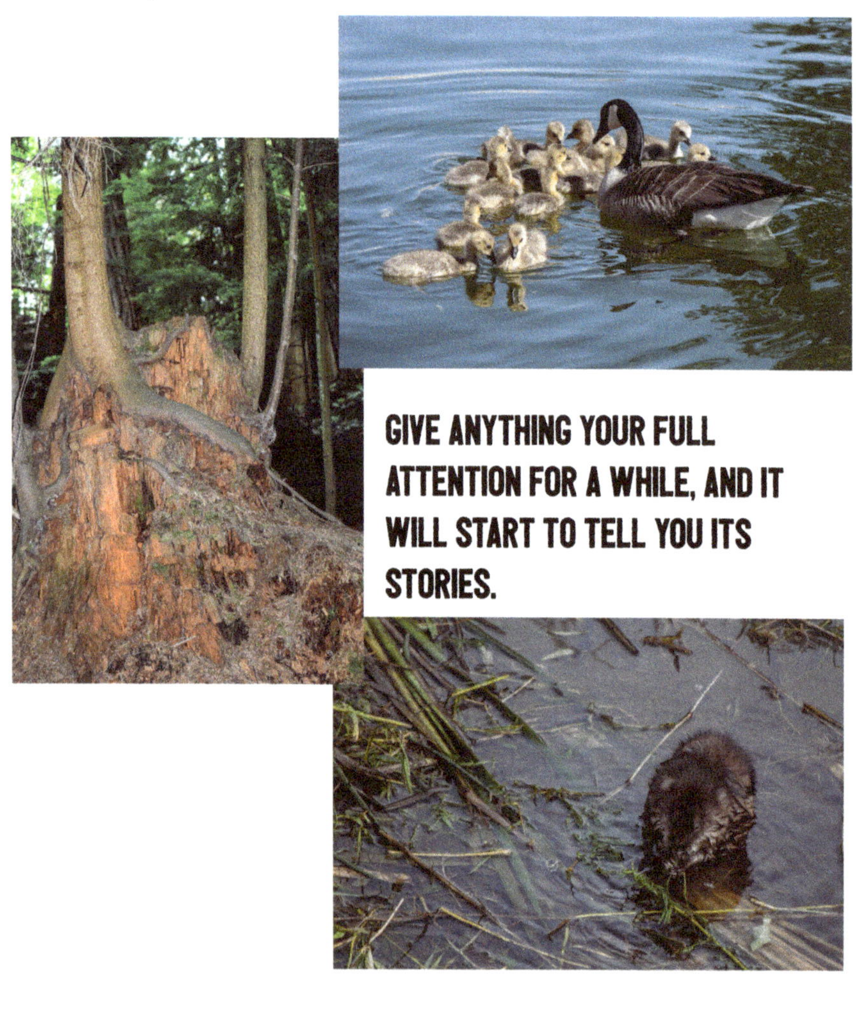

GIVE ANYTHING YOUR FULL ATTENTION FOR A WHILE, AND IT WILL START TO TELL YOU ITS STORIES.

With love to all my Facebook and Instagram friends,
who indulge my flights of fancy

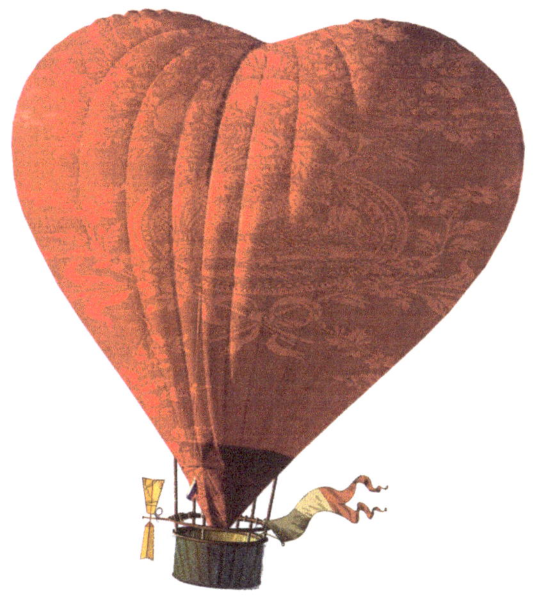

Special thanks to foxeysquirrel
for this delicious graphic

THE STORIES

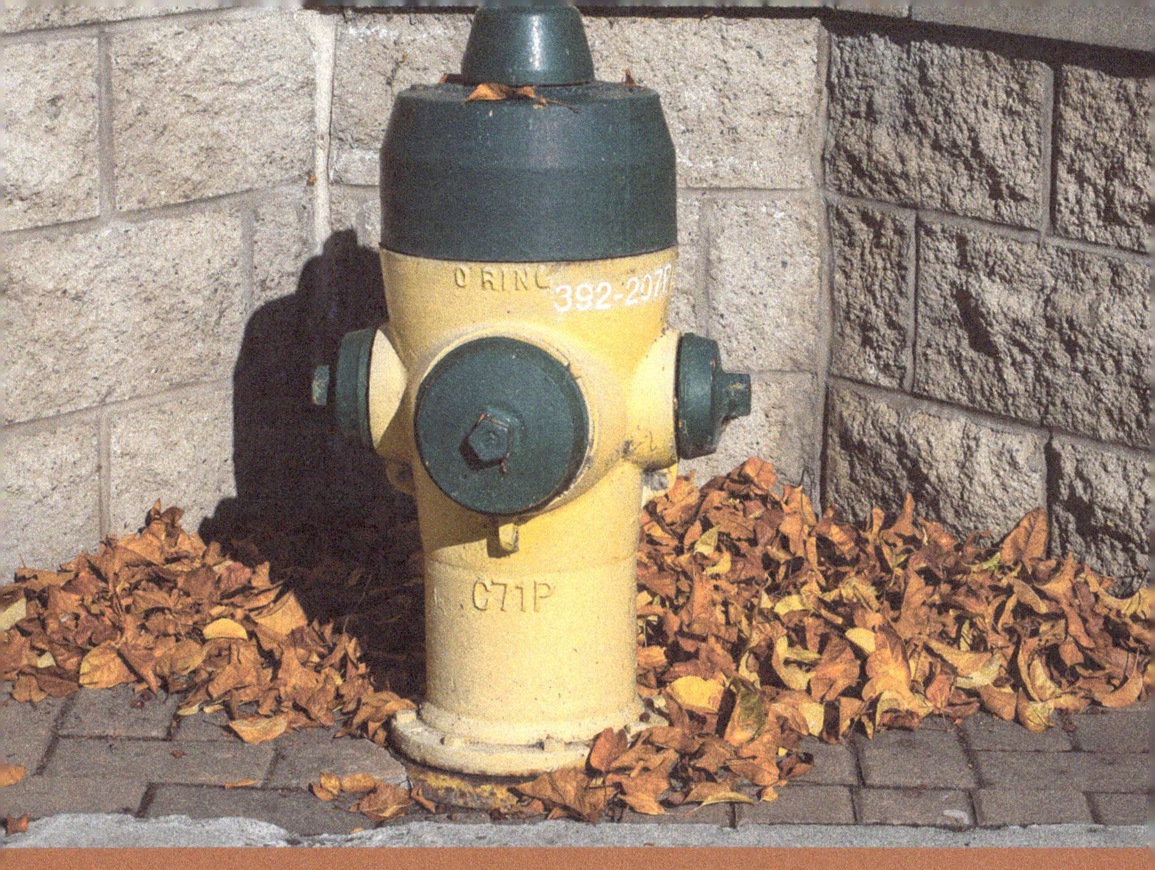

Hydrant was bursting with stories. All summer long he practiced them, knowing the time would come when Wind would surround him with dying leaves. They would welcome the solace of magical tales as they said farewell to their brief, beautiful lives.

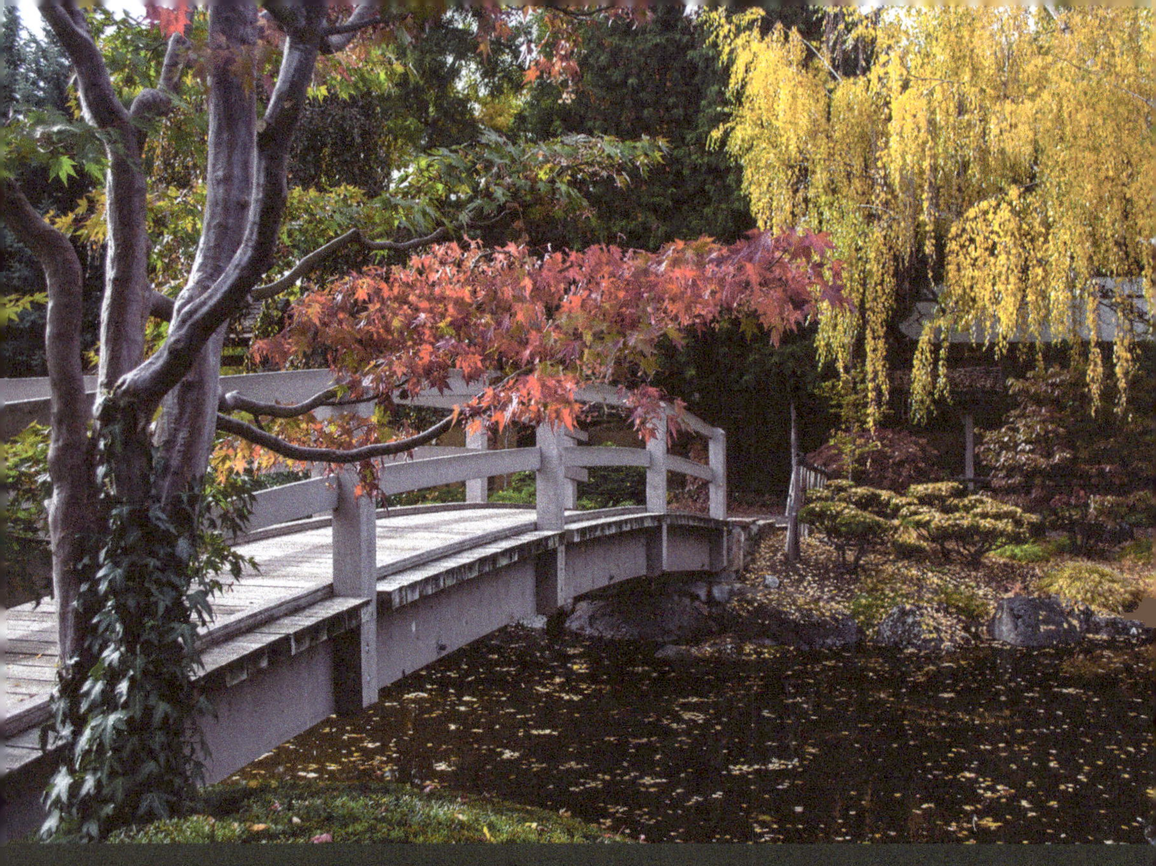

When the gates were locked for winter, Bridge invited his friends to shake it, shake it, shake it. Soon all the trees in the garden were bare of leaves, just in time for the Tree-Bones Ball.

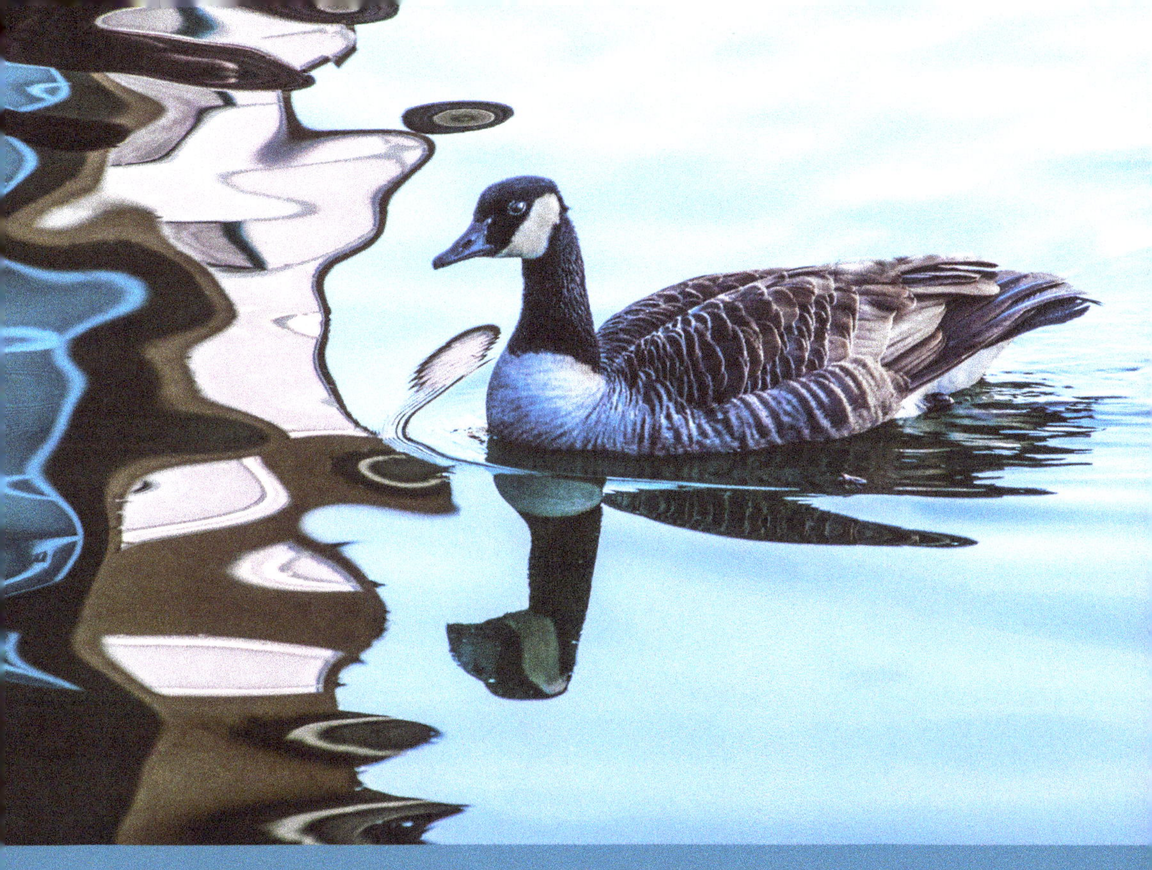

Goose was wide-eyed with surprise and delight. "Look at Water!" he honked to his mate. He is imitating my colors."

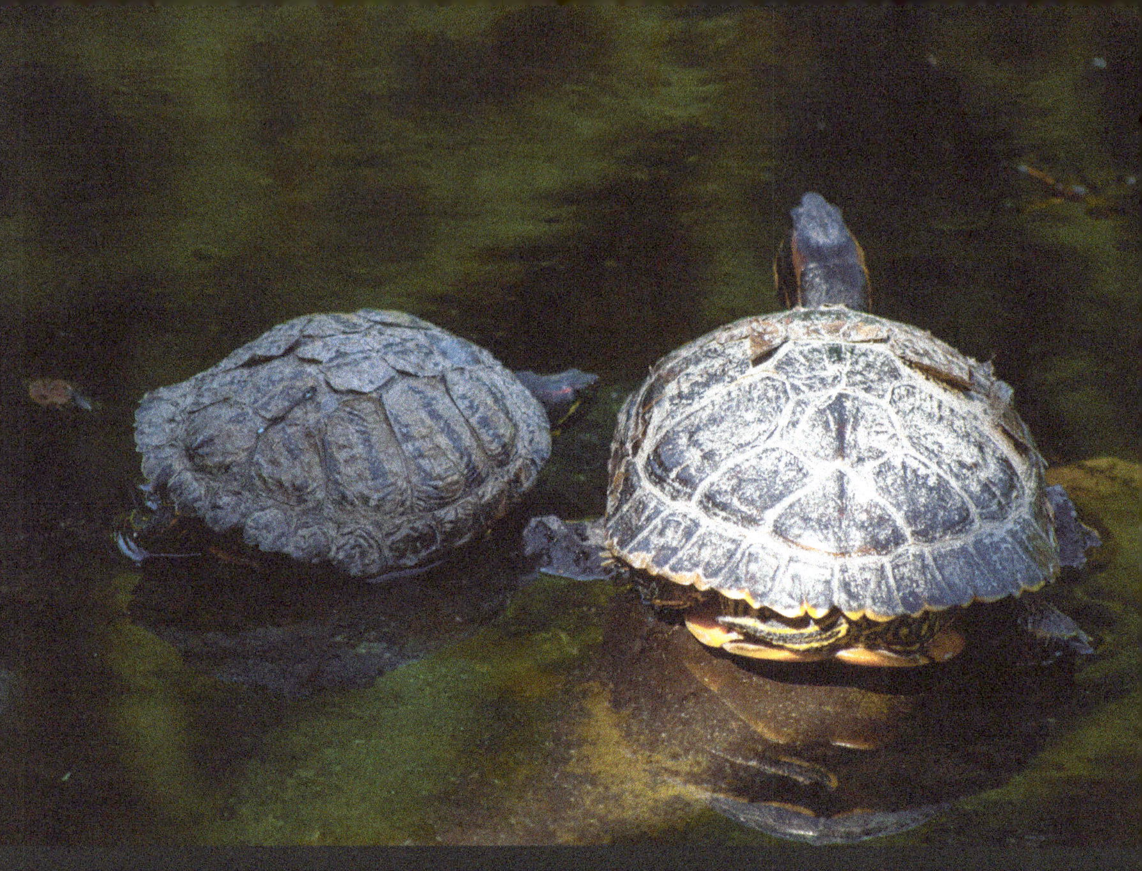

"Do you remember when..." asked Grandfather Turtle.

Grandmother Turtle sighed contentedly. Together they would re-tell stories of their younger years, when they were too busy to notice how quickly life passes.

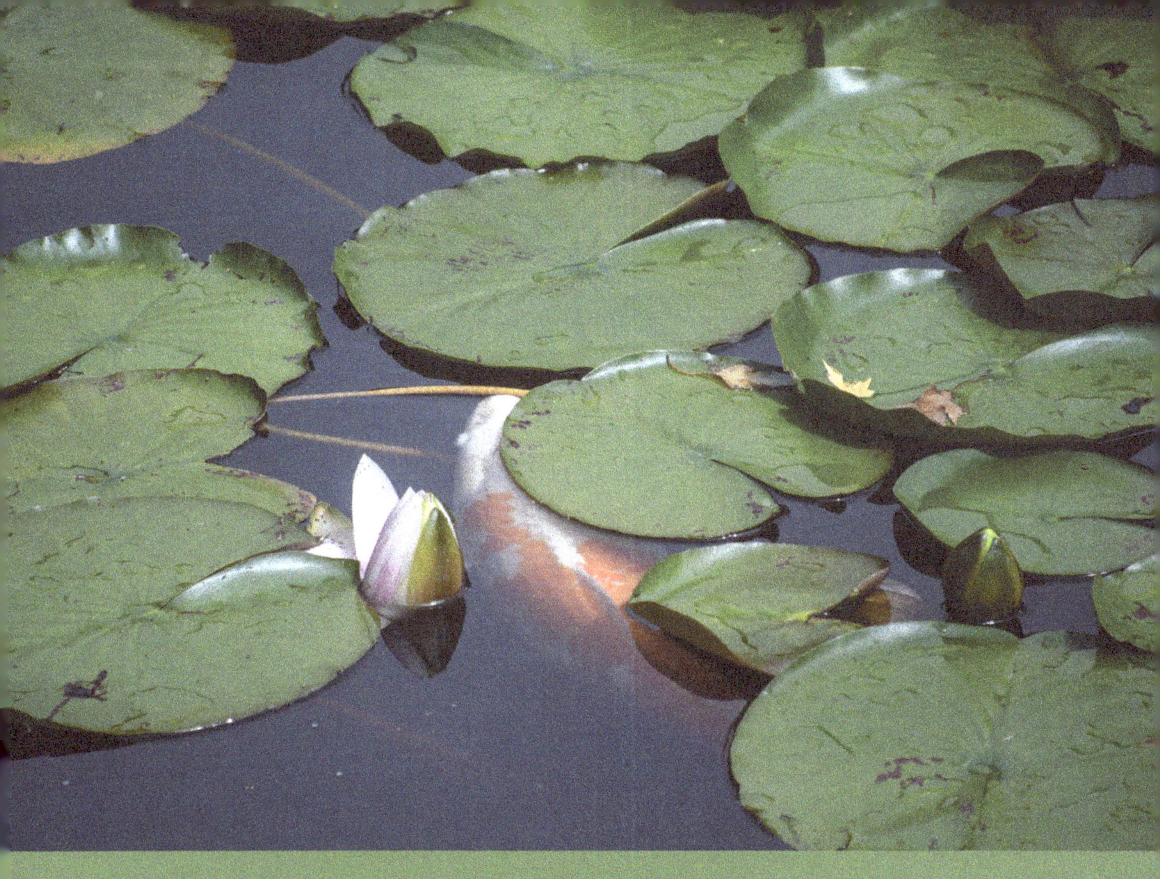

Koi loved to play hide-and-seek among the lily pads, but there was no use asking turtle for a game. All koi looked the same to him so he was always tagging the wrong one.

When her first
buds turned
into white
flowers, Lupine
felt awkward.
She was so
different from
her purple
friends. But as
her blossoms
shone in the
sun's light, she
laughed with
the joy of her
unique beauty.

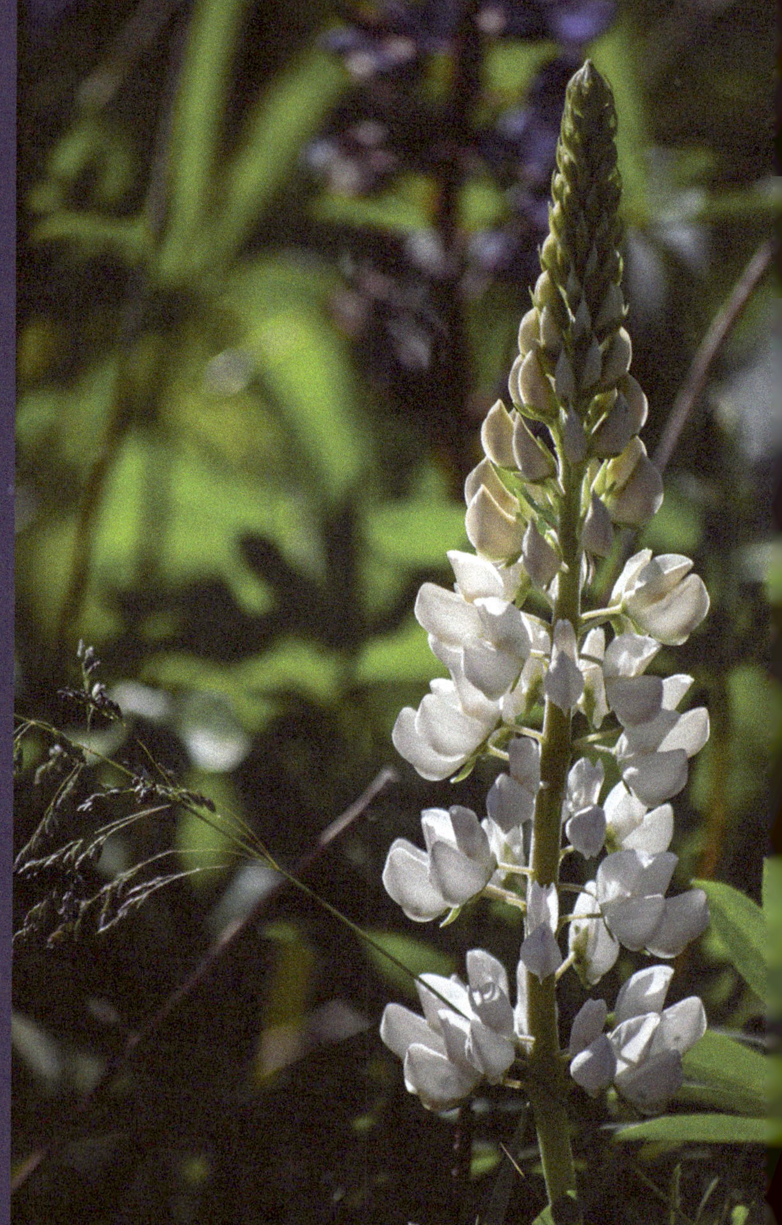

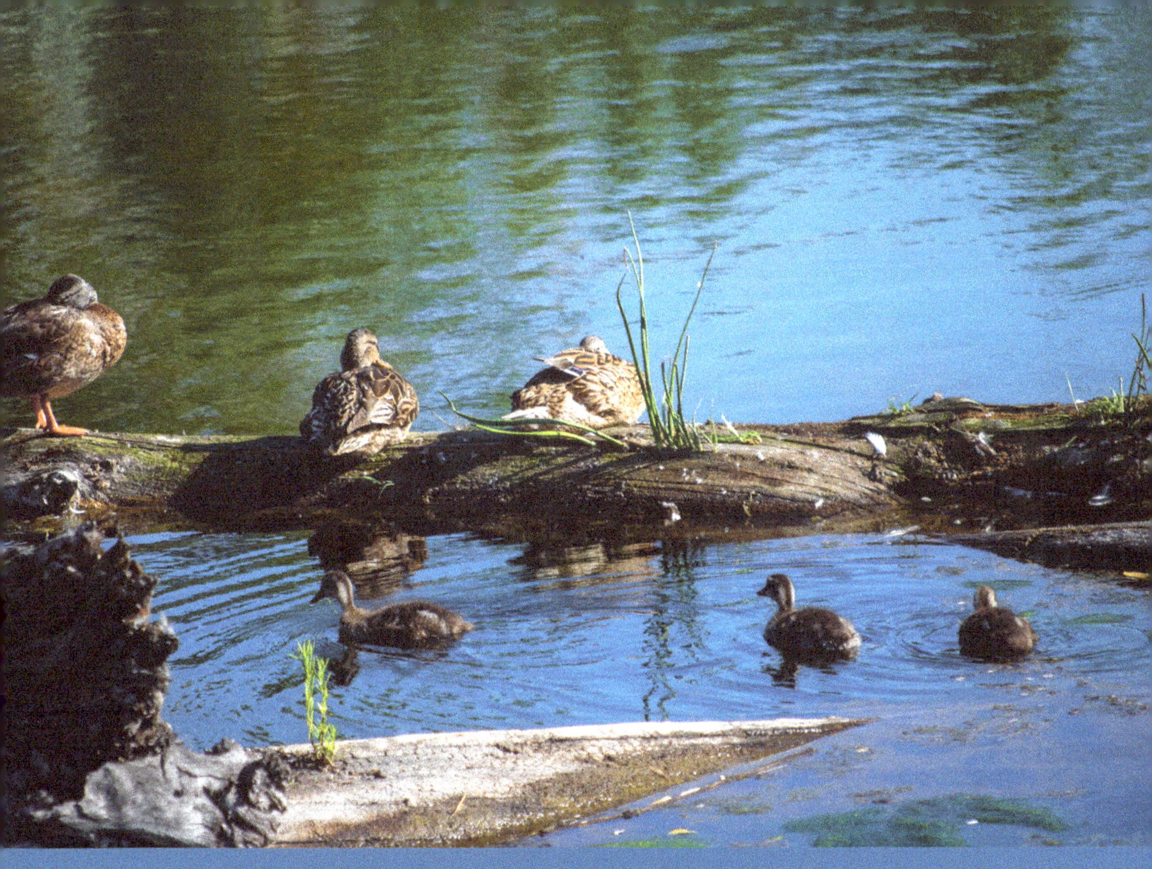

The youngsters woke her as they swam by, quacking loudly. "Why aren't you in school?" she grumbled.

"That's for fish," the ducklings laughed.

The twins
dressed alike
in every
season. As
they grew,
even their
trunks leaned
in the same
direction.
They could
not imagine
life without
each other.

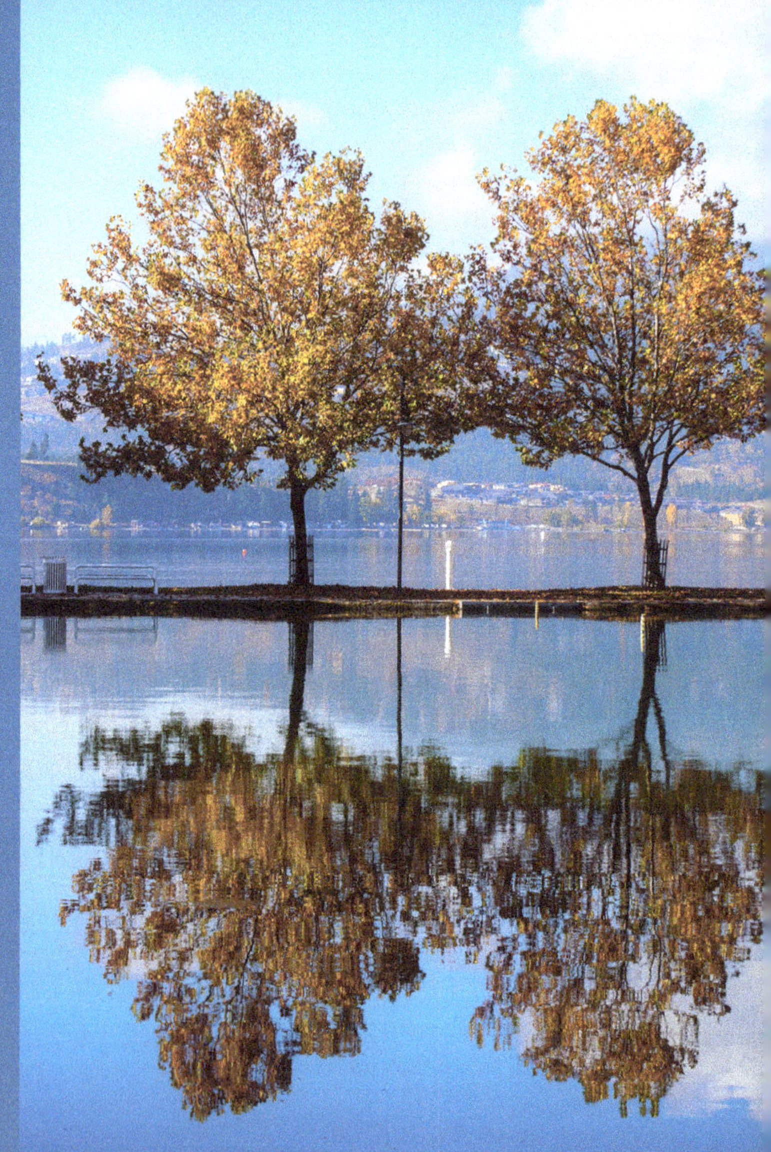

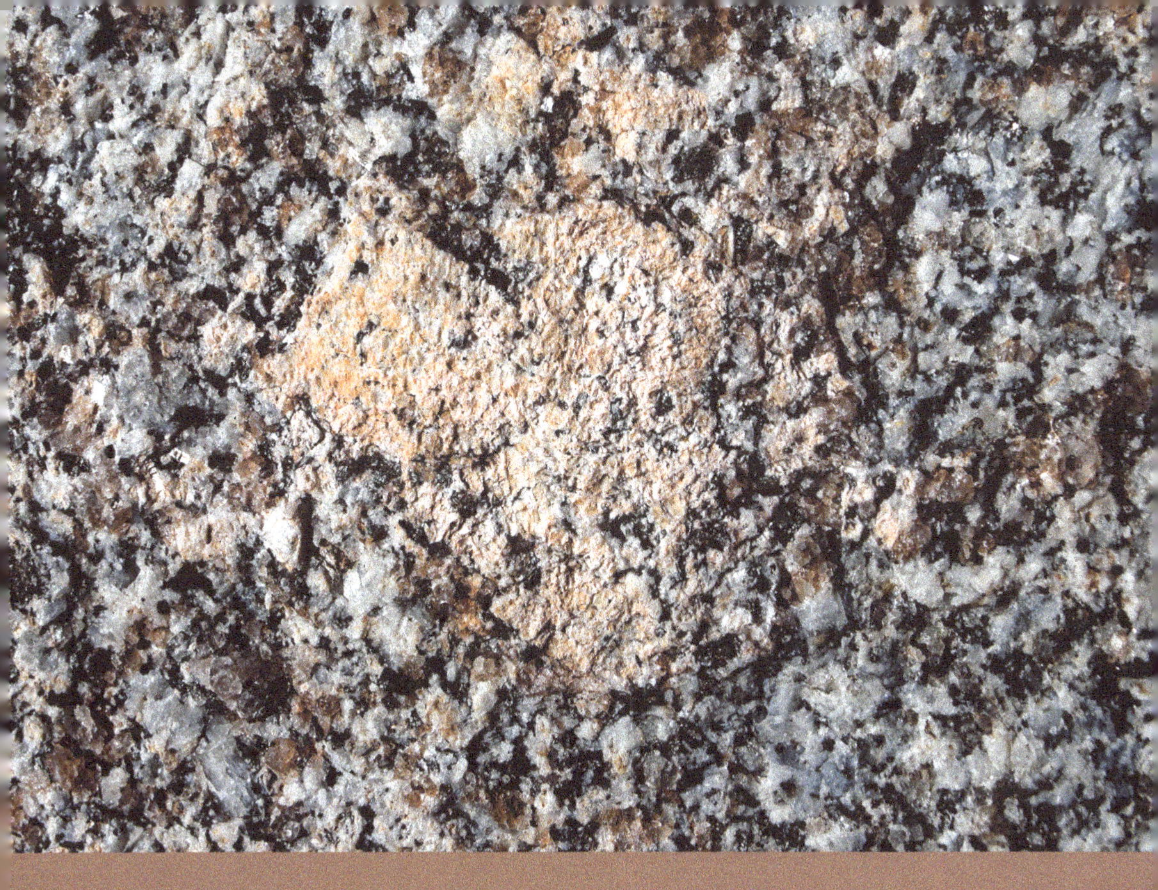

Earth Mama planted love hearts everywhere.
She was not seeking recognition. She was telling
every flower and rock, every bird and river, every
human and tree how much she loved them.

The two seed clusters whispered and planned. They moved together just right, forming eyes and what they hoped was a scary face. They were sorry no one screamed, but they still liked the game.

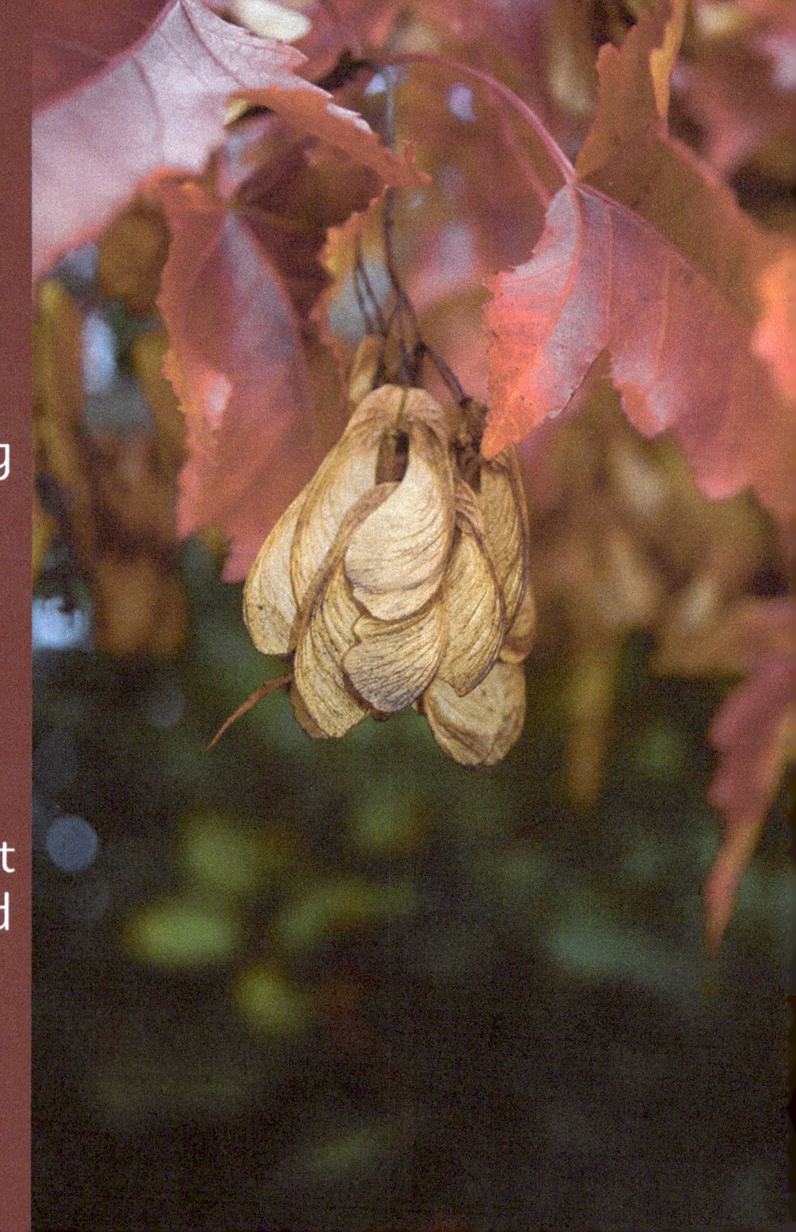

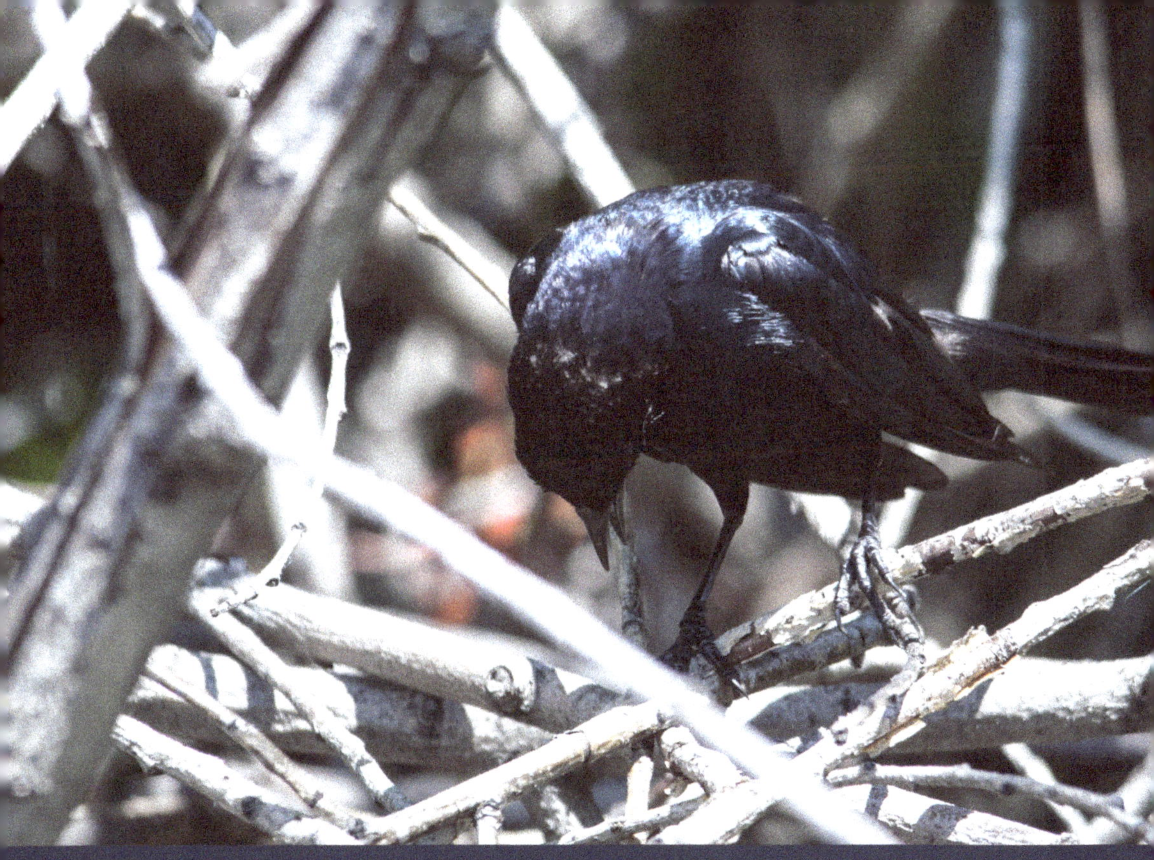

The Brewer's Blackbird looked down in dismay. "My seed! I dropped my seed. It was the best seed ever. I'll never find another one like it. This is the worst day EVER."

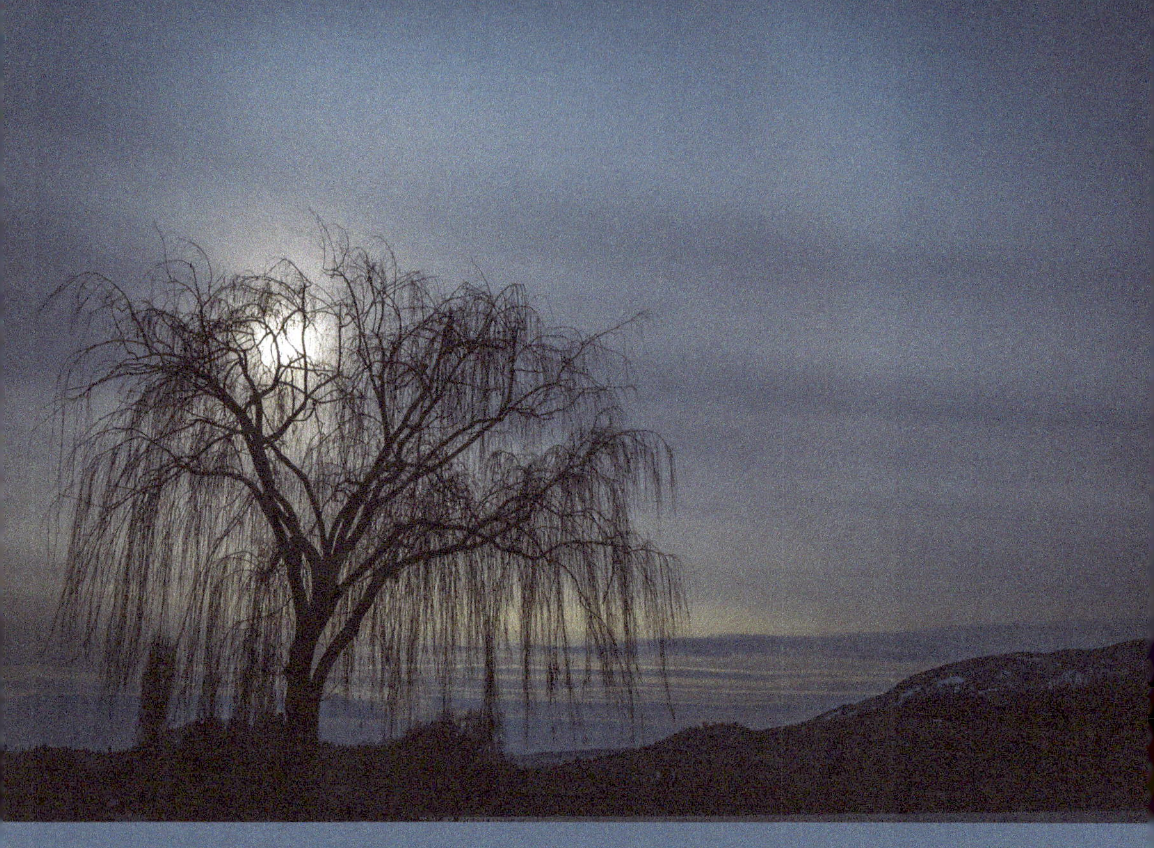

"Uh, oh. Sky's in a mood," groaned Willow. She could see the rainbow ring and knew a storm was coming.

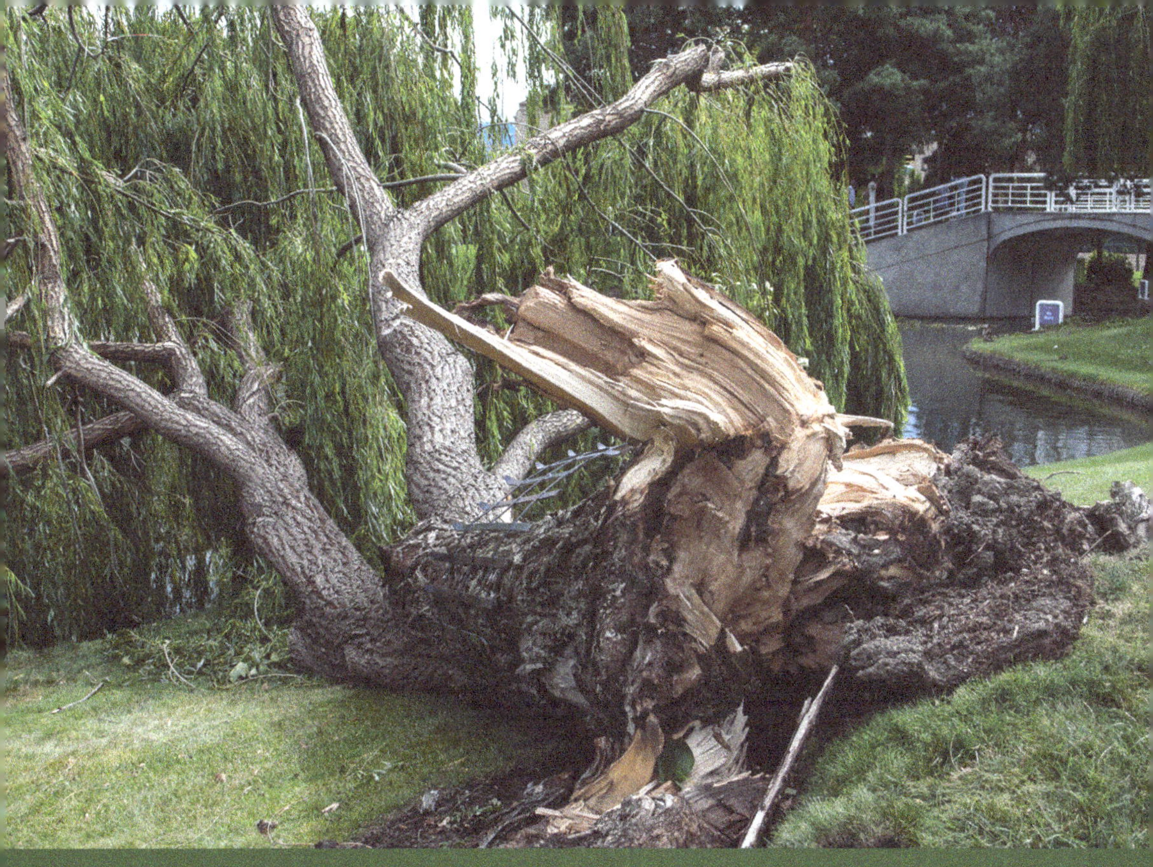

Wind was sad. He had only wanted to play with Willow. He had forgotten how strong he was. Now she would never play with him again.

Elephant Tree smiled. The child had stood and stared at him. When he offered to tell her a story, he saw her eyes light up. She nodded eagerly and spoke to him in tree language. He hoped she would come again. He knew many stories.

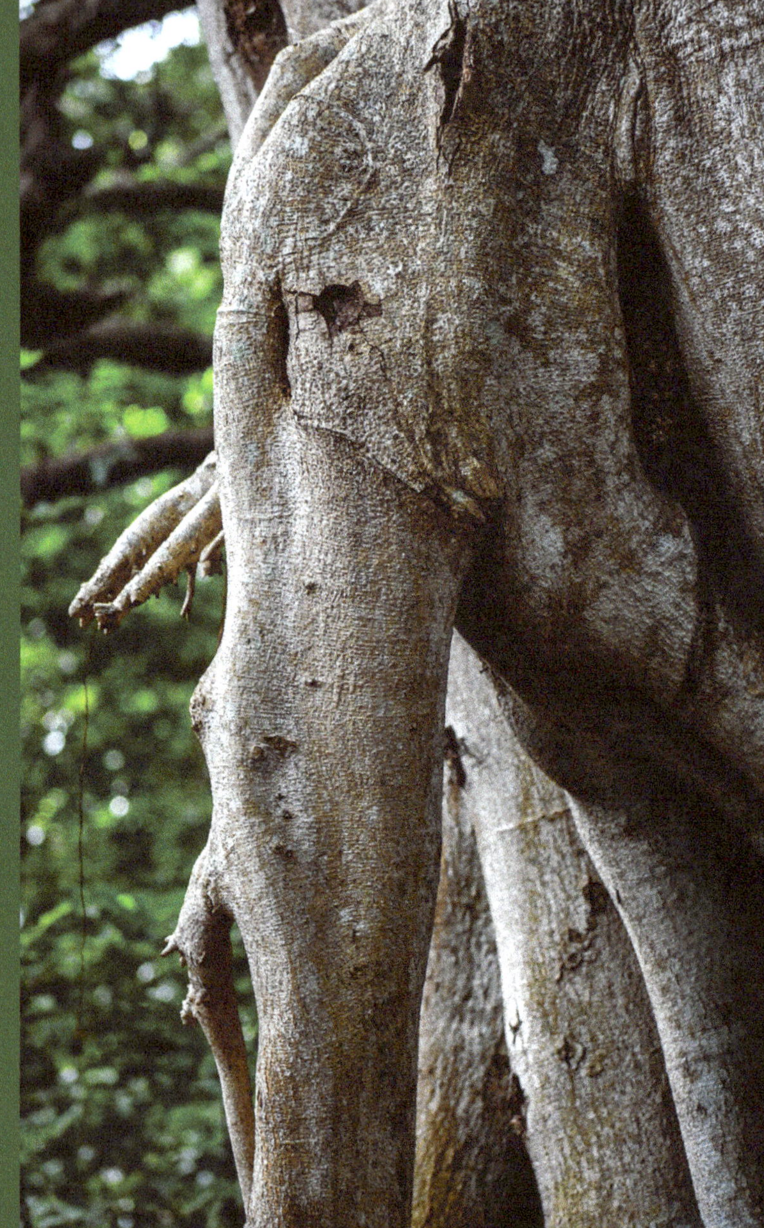

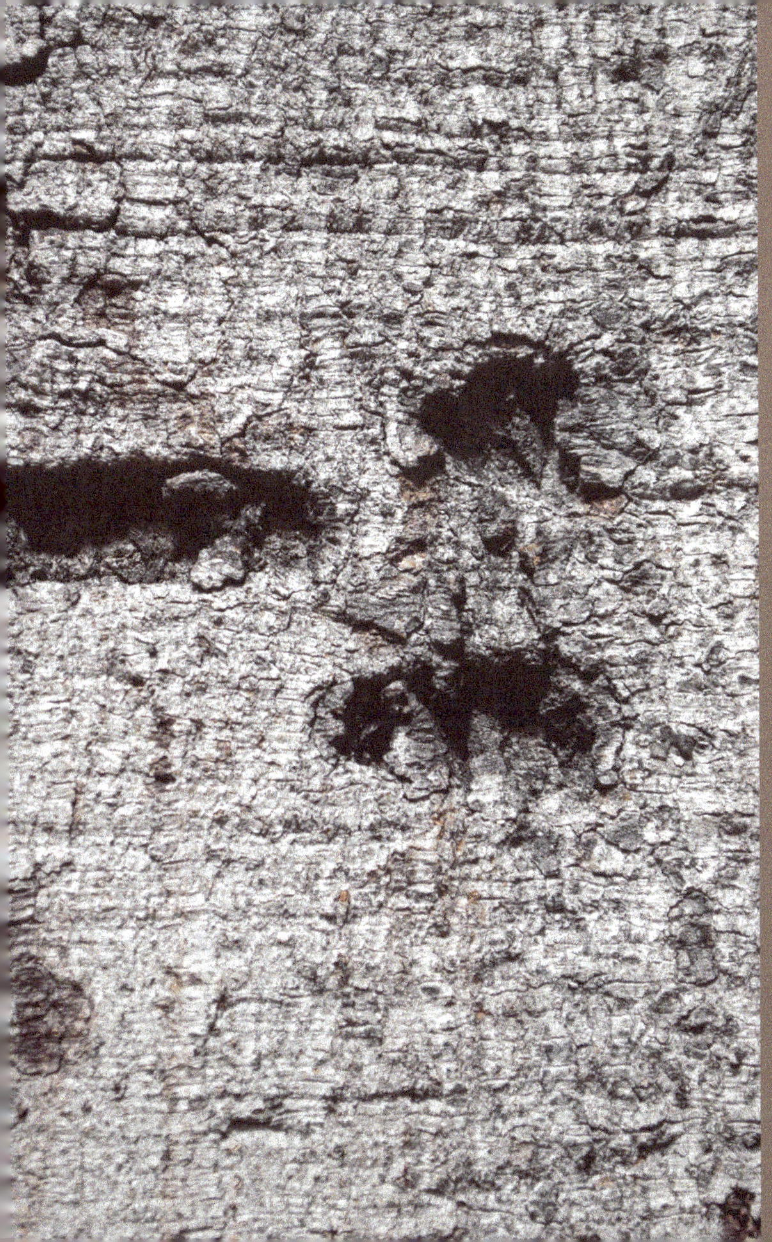

Tree Man was the strong, silent type. As an introvert, he was happy just to look wise and not have to make small talk.

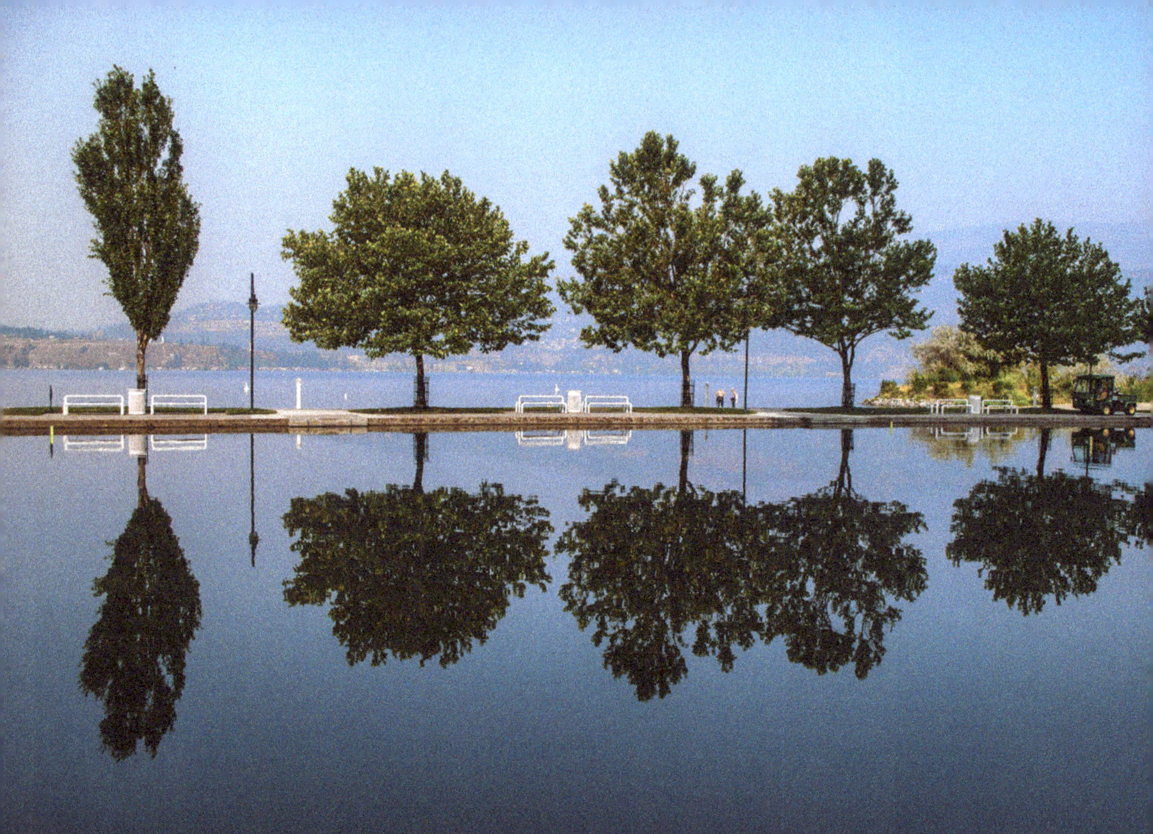

The tree family loved still days, when their reflections on the lagoon were perfect. But they held their breaths, knowing Wind would soon swoop down to tease them.

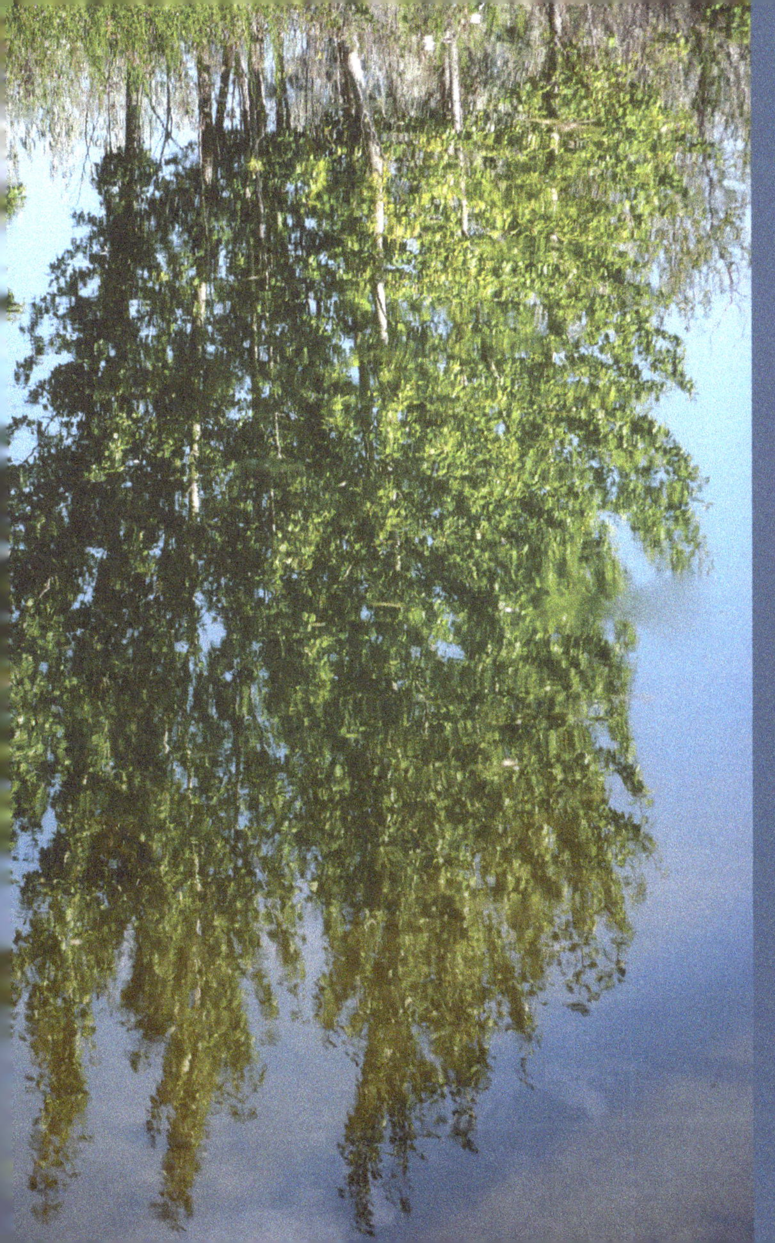

Trees looked at their reflections in the marsh and laughed. "Hold still, Breeze. We're going to fool the humans."

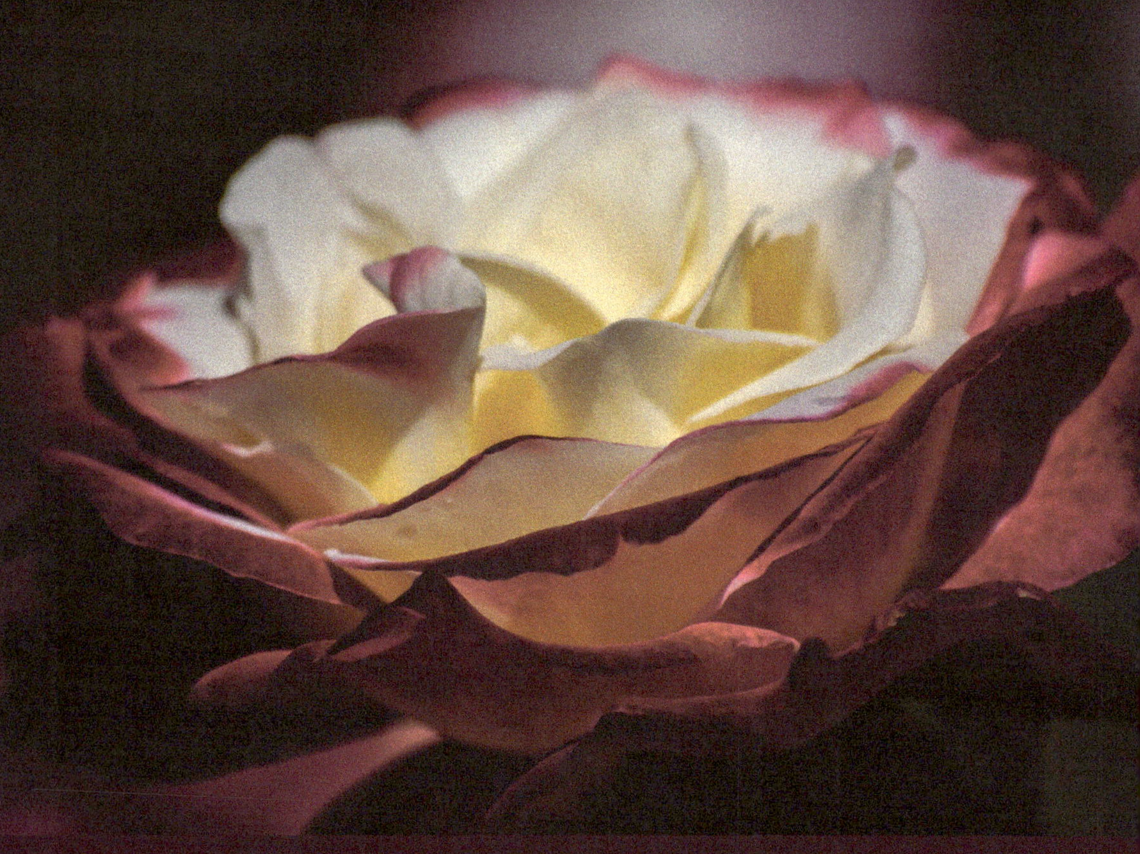

People and insects leaned into her vibrant depths, intoxicated by her heady fragrance. She was blithely unaware of her effect on them. She never thought of herself as exceptional.

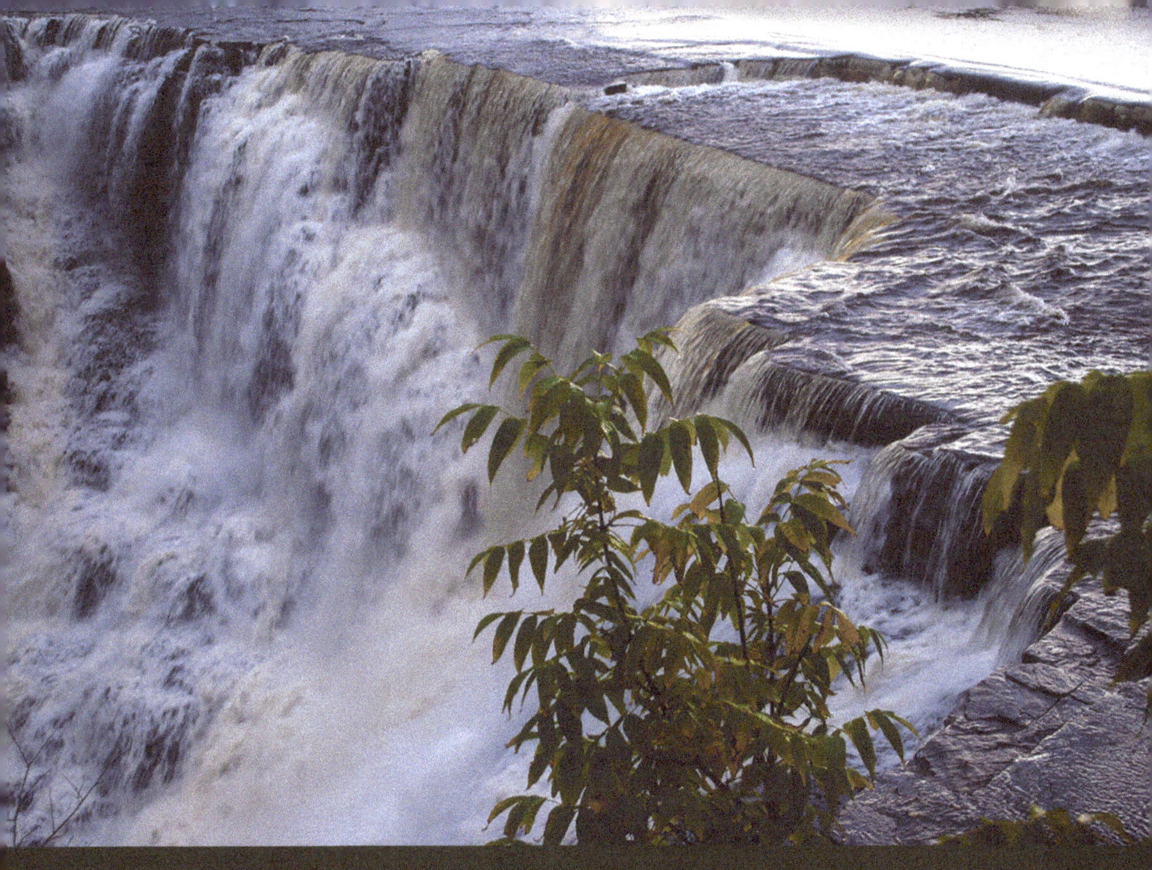

Water loved racing between canyons and resting through farm fields. Nothing was more exciting than a steep drop-off, where he could thunder mightily and scare the bejeebers out of kayakers.

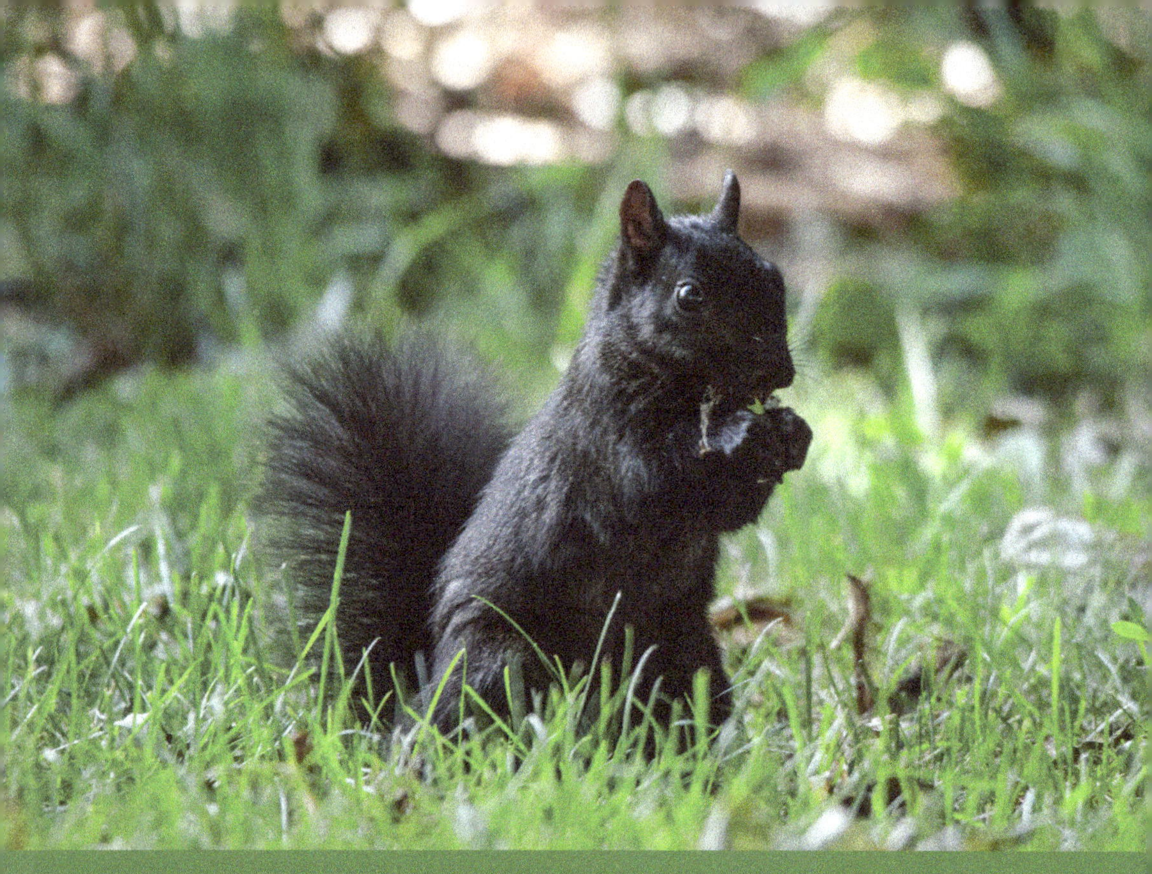

Black Squirrel knew he was supposed to concentrate on gathering nuts for winter. But Wind played with his tail. Crow dropped nuts nearby. Sun peeked through tree limbs. The world was far too amazing to ignore.

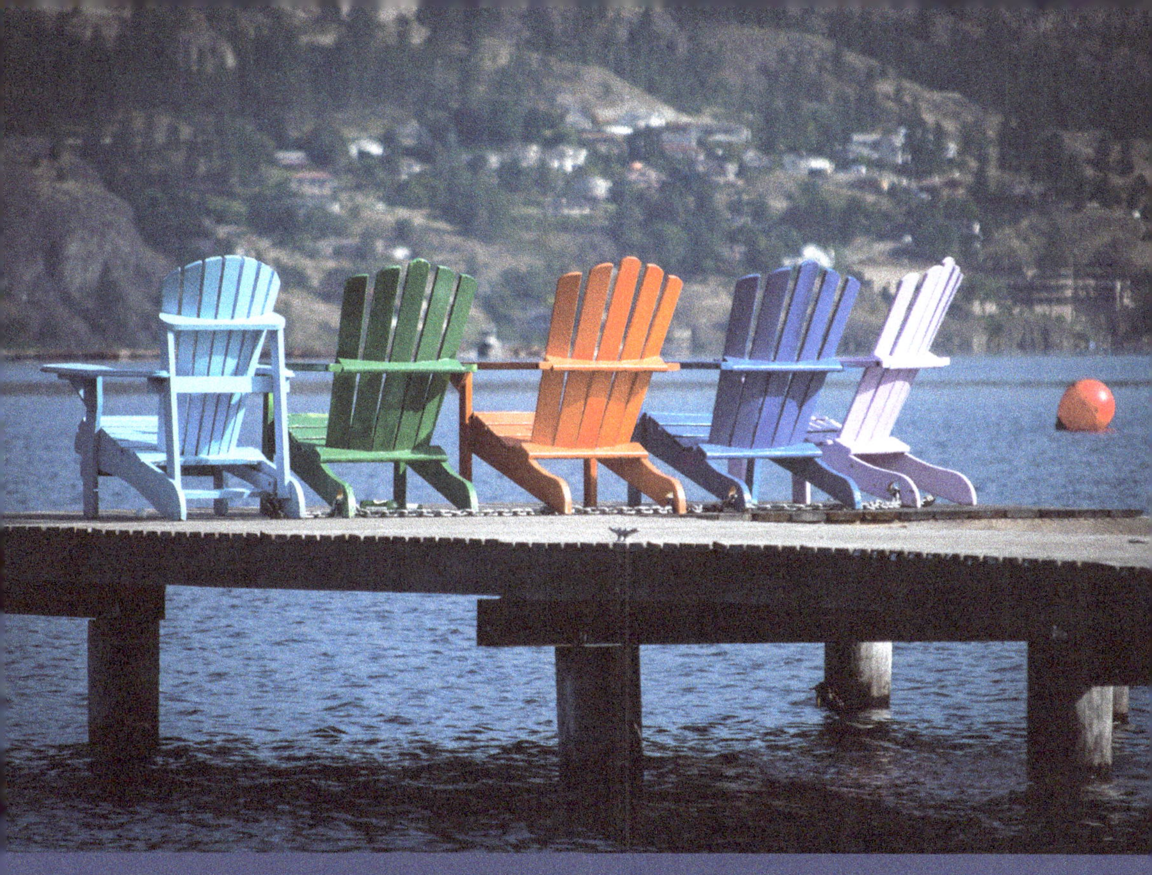

Chairs loved this time of year, when the Summer People took them out of storage and lined them up where they could look out at the lake.

"Oh, you doll," Tree said, as Sun lit the leaf bouquet at her feet. She understood the light was his gift to her. Her enthusiasm made Sun beam all the brighter.

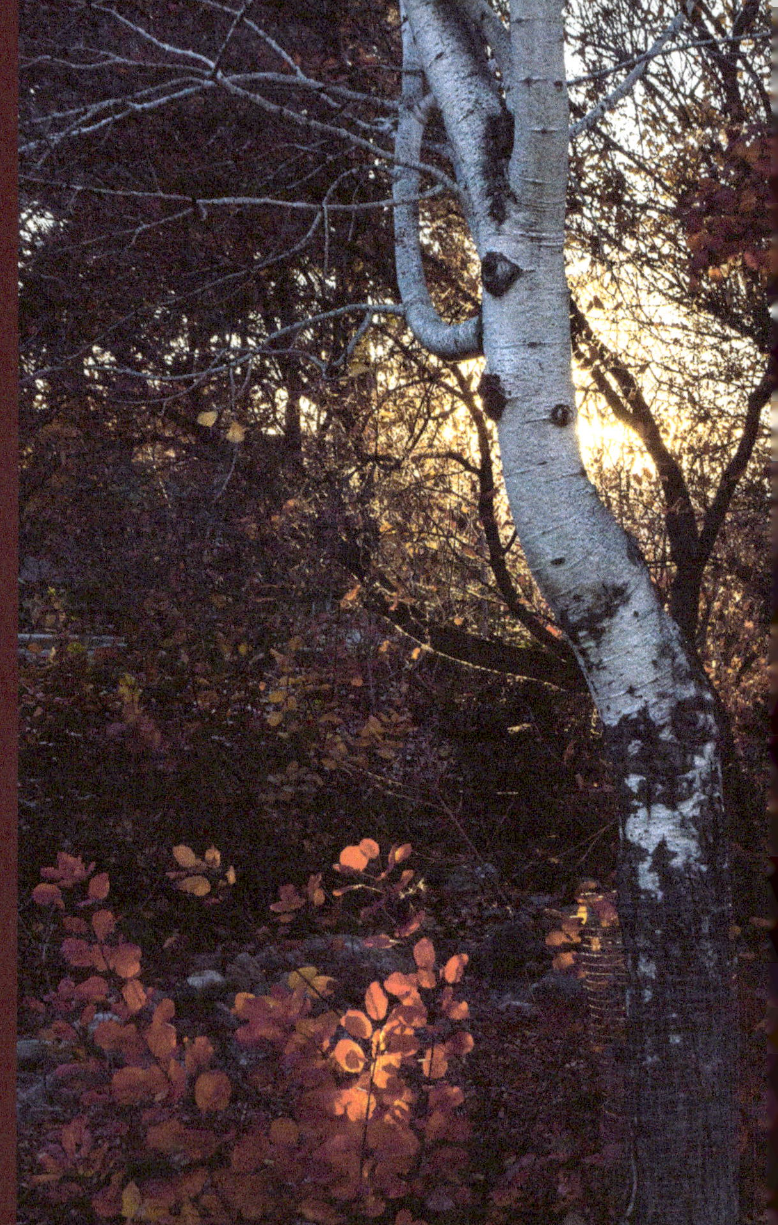

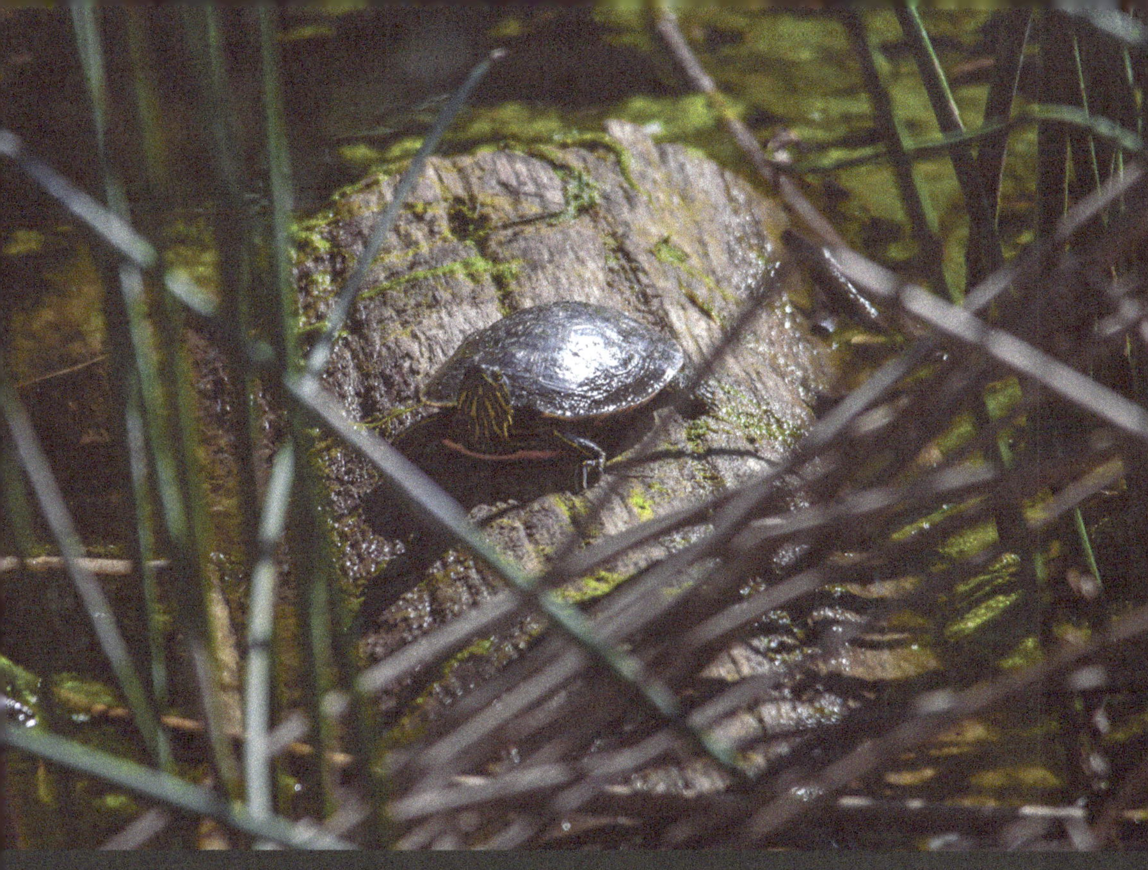

Small Turtle stared at the tall stalks of the reeds. He looked at the algae growing close around his favourite log. He felt a delicious shiver of fear and began making up stories about dark forests and ravenous monsters.

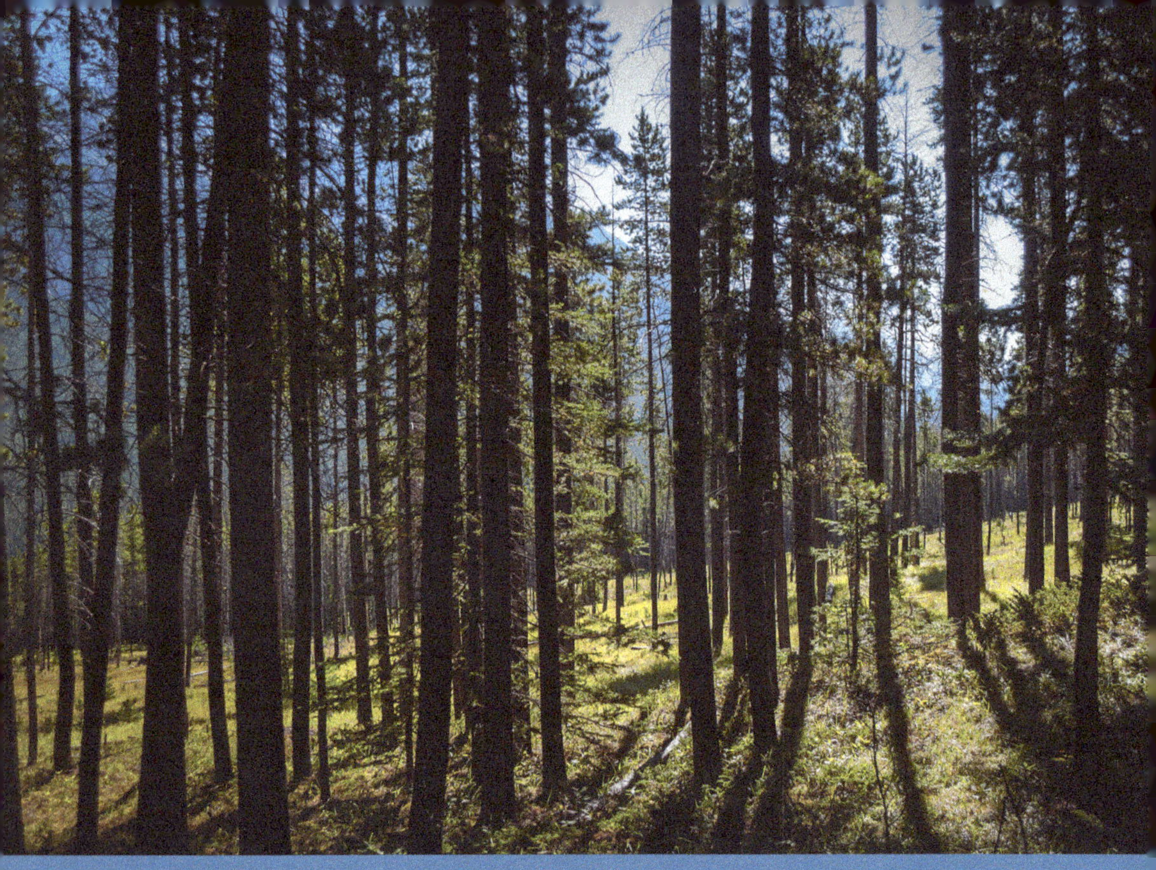

Sun played with the grass and caressed the tree trunks. "We love you, Sun," cried the trees. "You make us look so beautiful." Sun beamed all the brighter. He knew the trees made him visible.

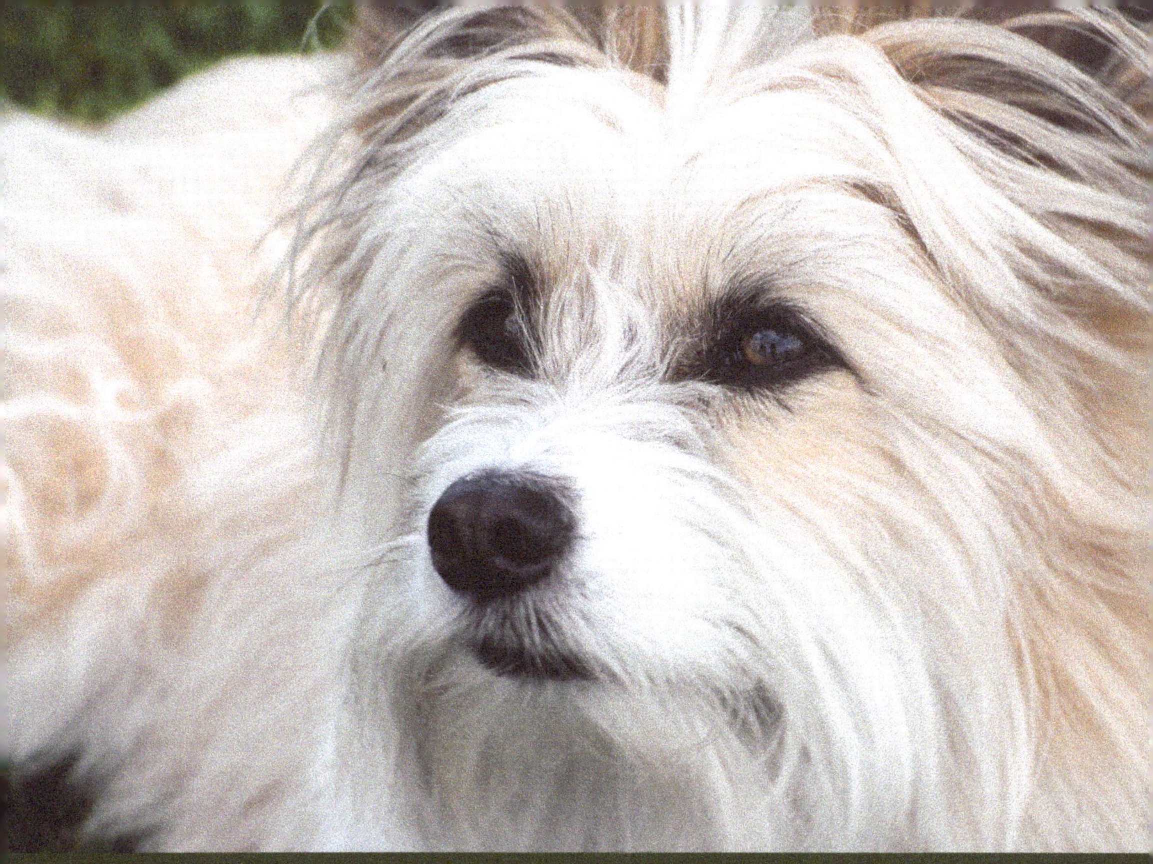

Max gazed at her fondly. She was his companion, his provider, his best and truest friend. With only two legs and a head so far off the ground, she missed much of what he knew about the world he smelled so freely. He loved her anyway.

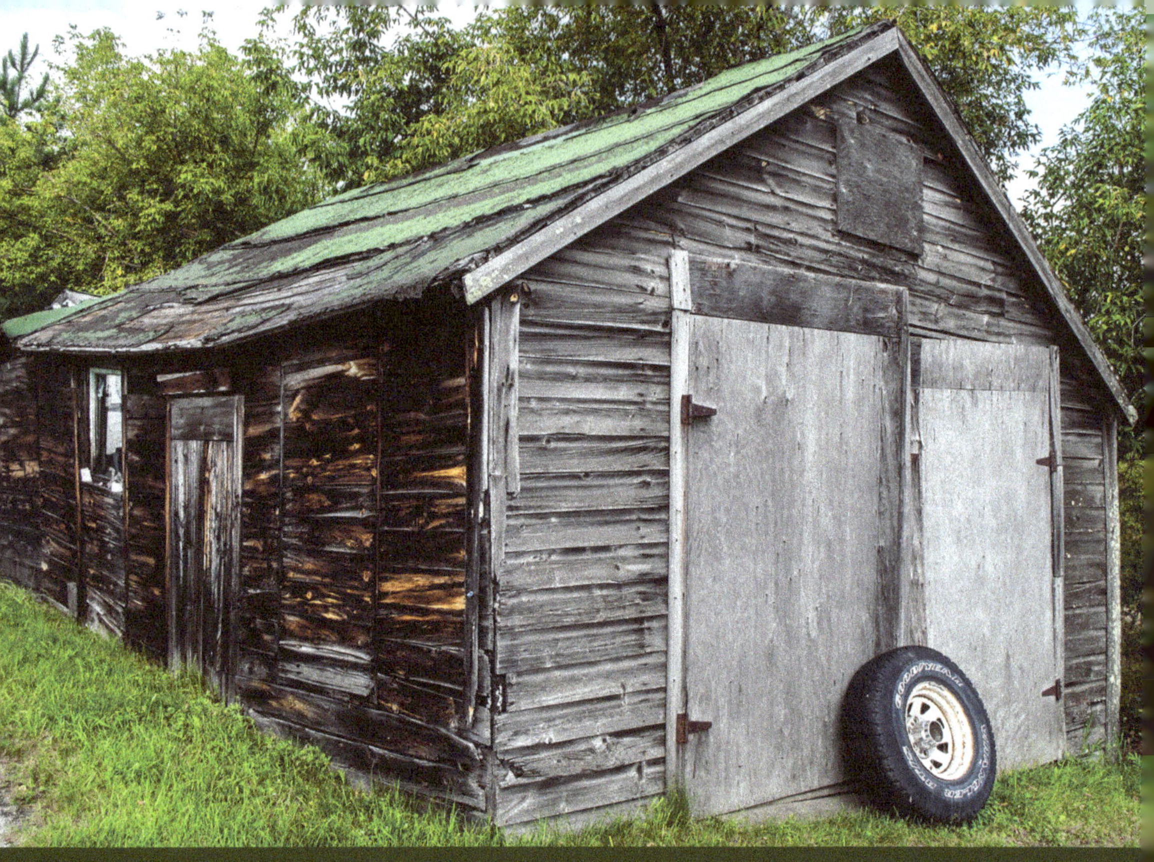

Her roof sagged. She was badly in need of a coat of paint. If anyone moved the tire, her doors would swing open. But Shed was happy. In her day she had sheltered tools, work benches, and a valuable car. She was proud of her years of service.

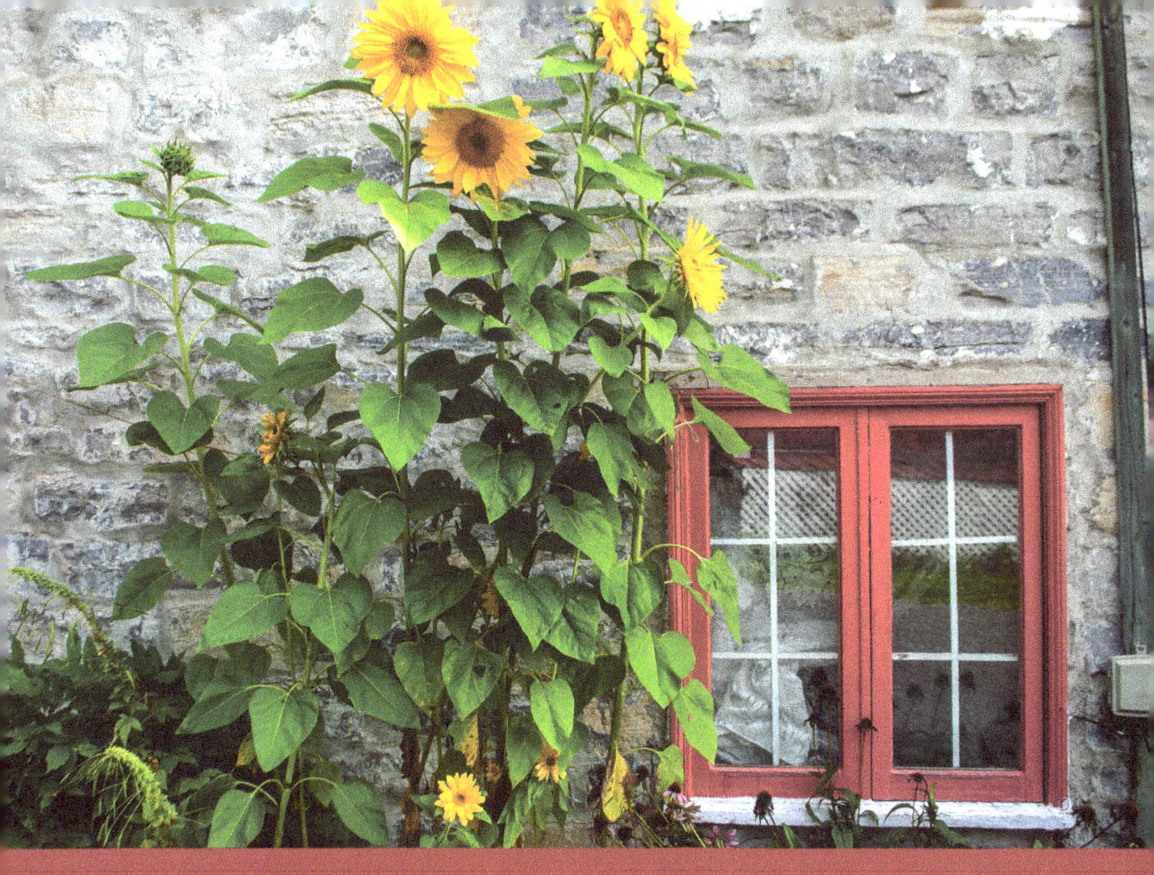

Window loved her summer friends. House Woman planted the seeds every spring, but she never heard the stories Window and Sunflowers whispered to each other all summer. Their secrets were delicious.

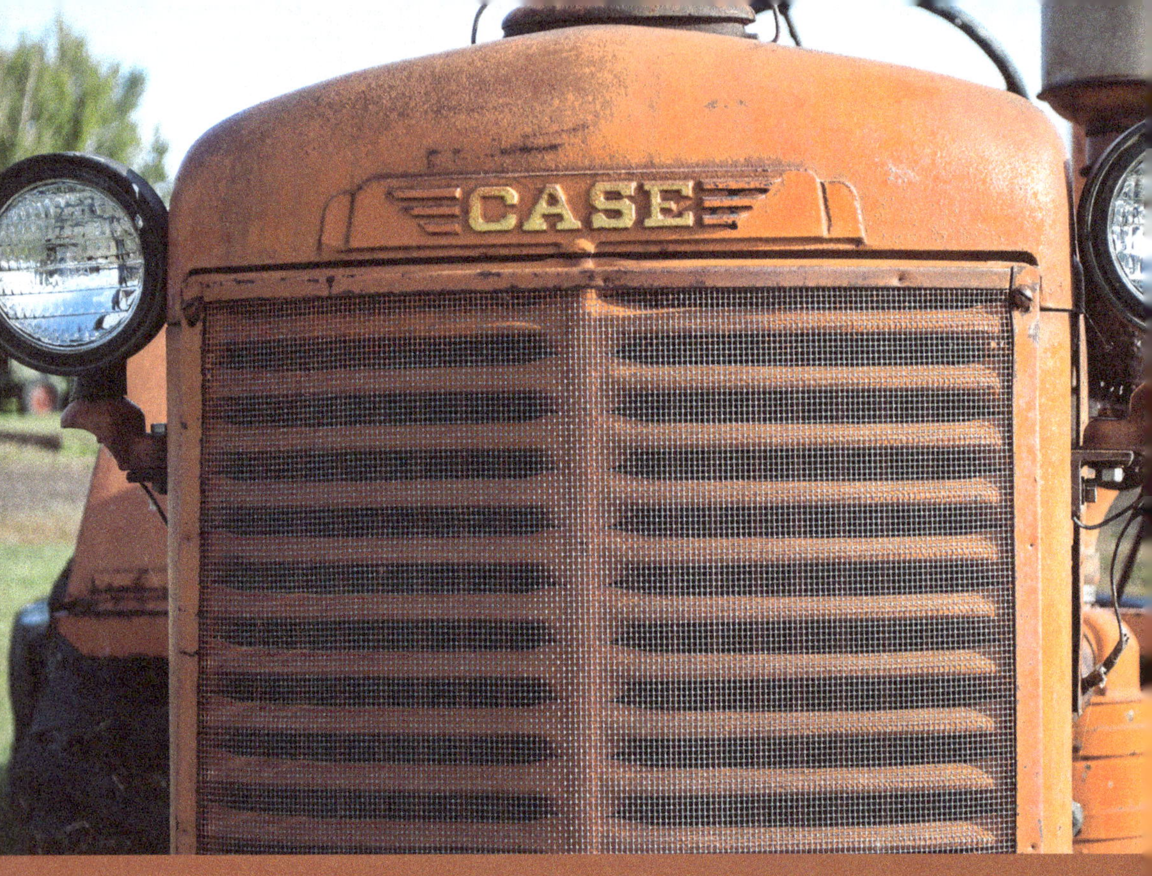

"In Case you hadn't noticed, I'm orange," said the old tractor, snorting with laughter. It was his only pun, and not a good one, but his friends always laughed politely.

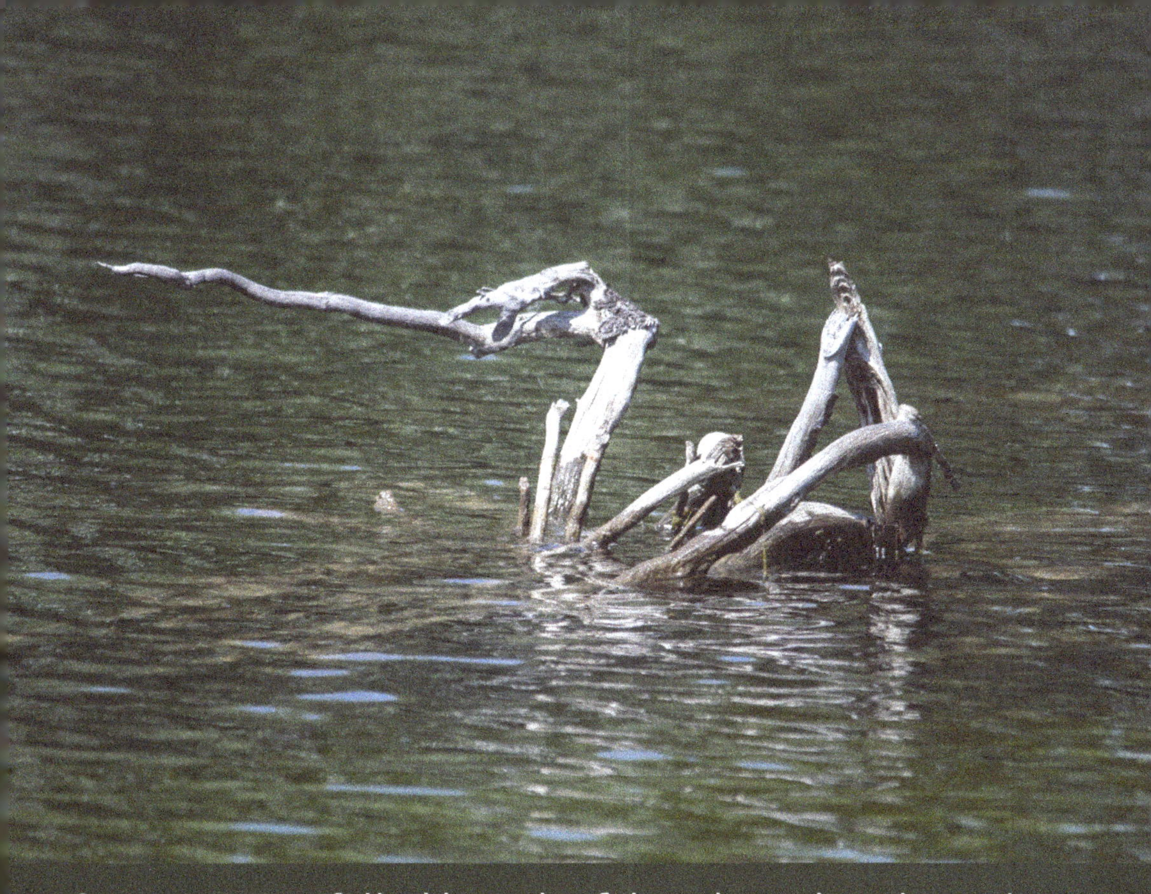

After Saw Man felled her, she felt ugly and useless. Then Park Guy tossed her in a marsh. Water, Sun and Wind bleached and twisted her. Now she loved life again. She played many roles - unicorn, sea monster, driving woman with streaming hair. She never ran out of ideas.

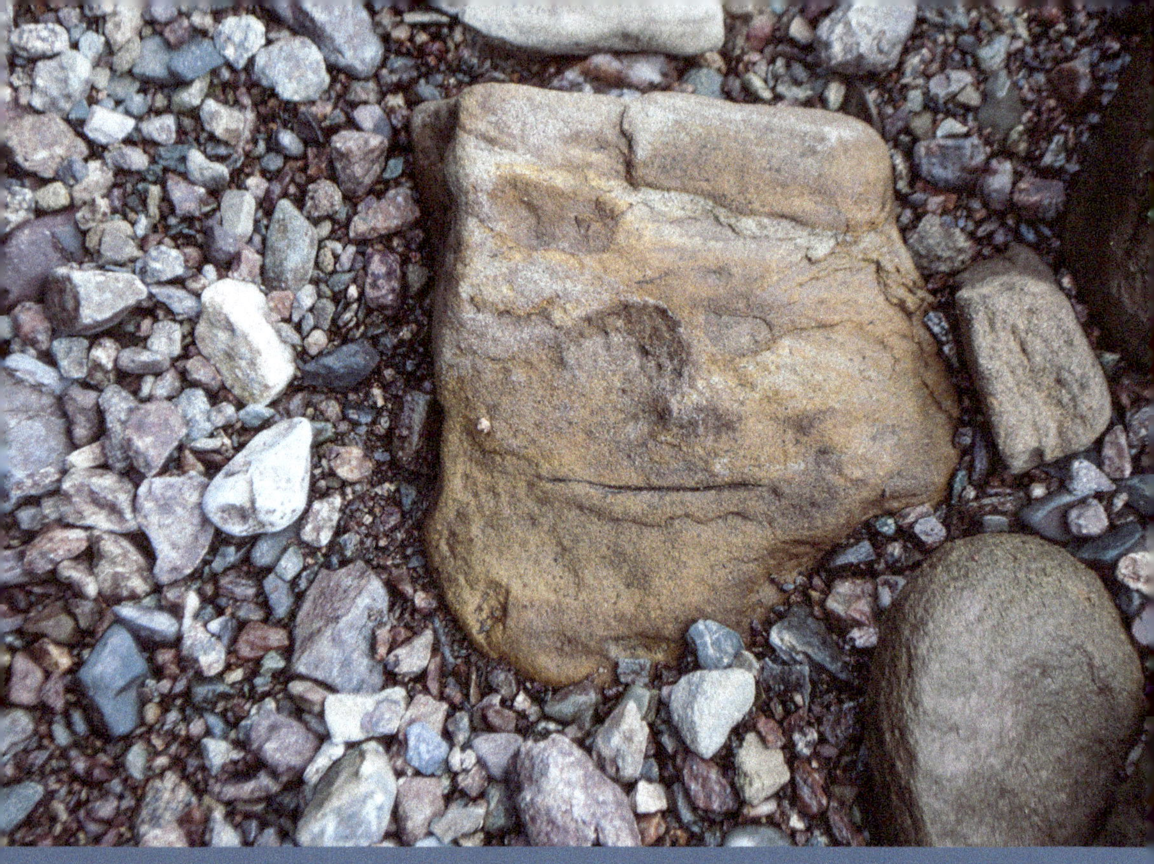

Rock Man waited patiently, through twice-daily tides, through seasons and storms, through sun bright and moonlight. Some day, he knew, someone would see his intelligent face and take him home. Rock Man longed for that friend.

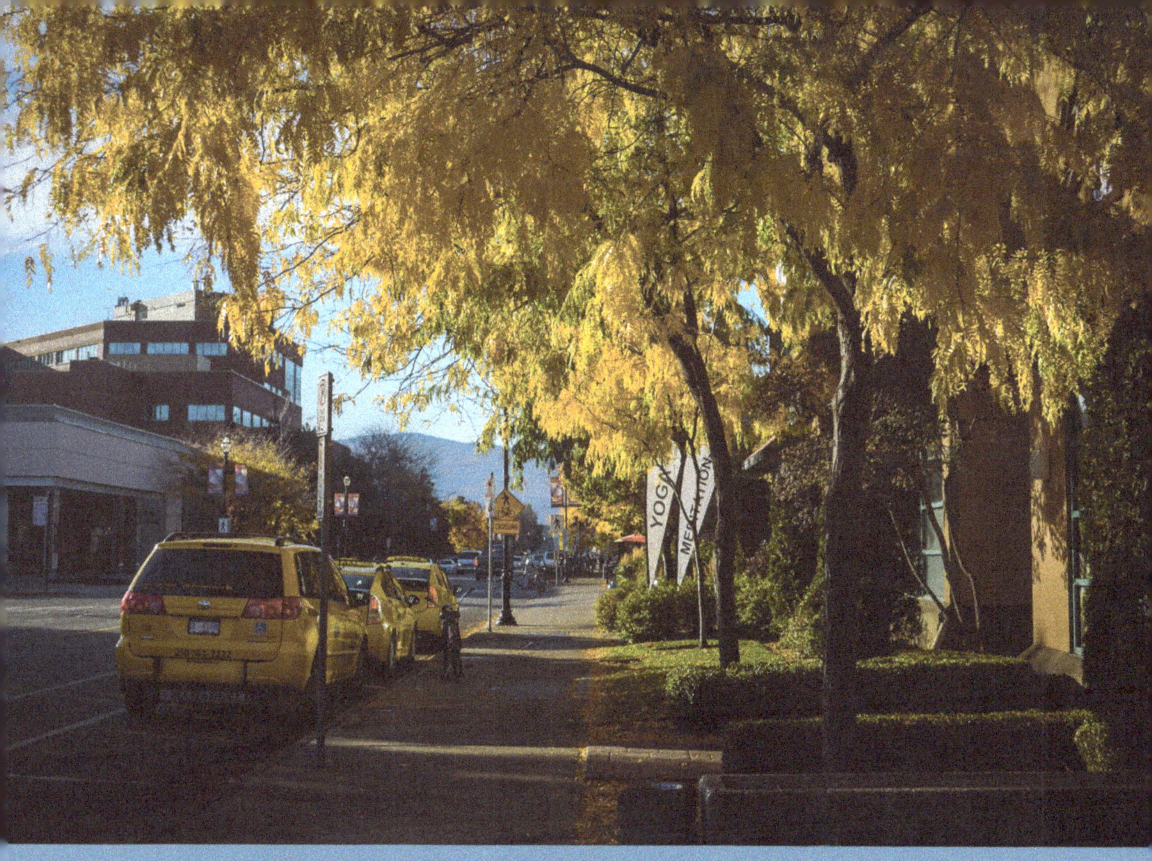

The drivers didn't know it, but their taxis had been plotting with the trees all summer. As soon as leaves changed in autumn, they made a Big Yellow Splash.

Decades had passed since she tenderly wrapped her small roots around Grandfather Tree and vowed to look after him forever. Now she was a Grandmother Tree, sharing the lessons of her ancestors with the seedlings and young trees around her.

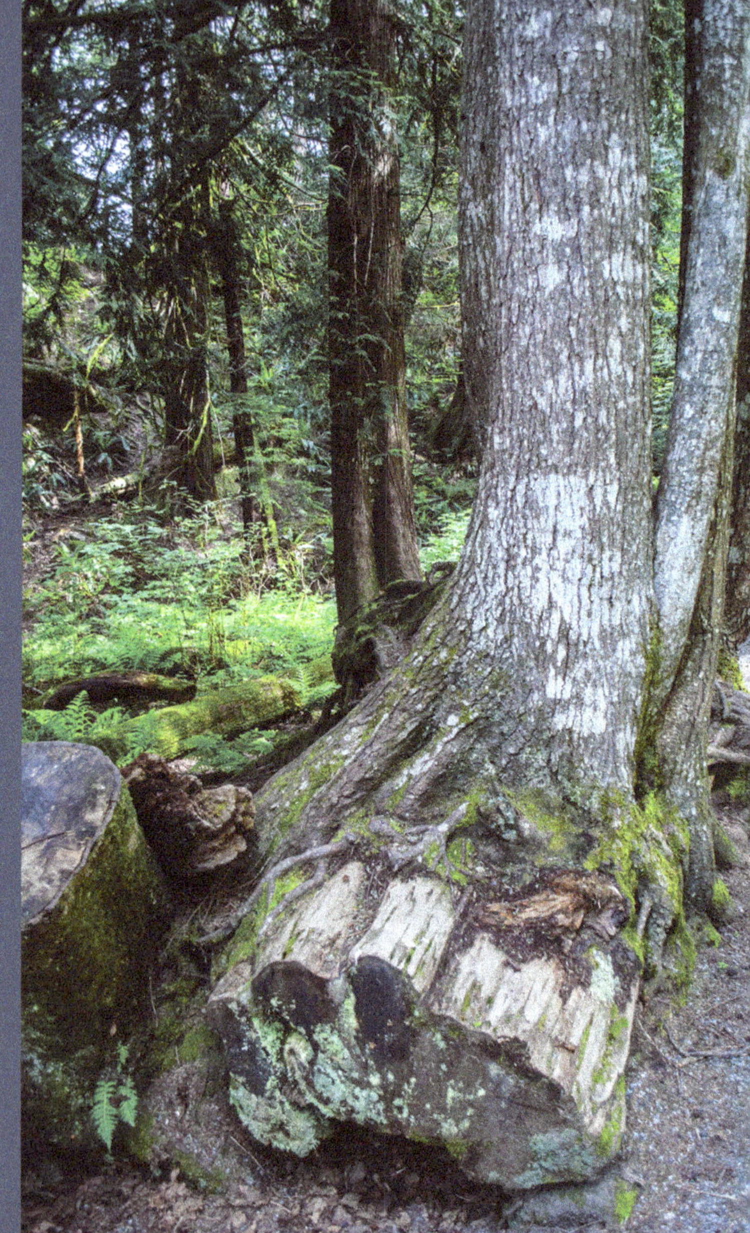

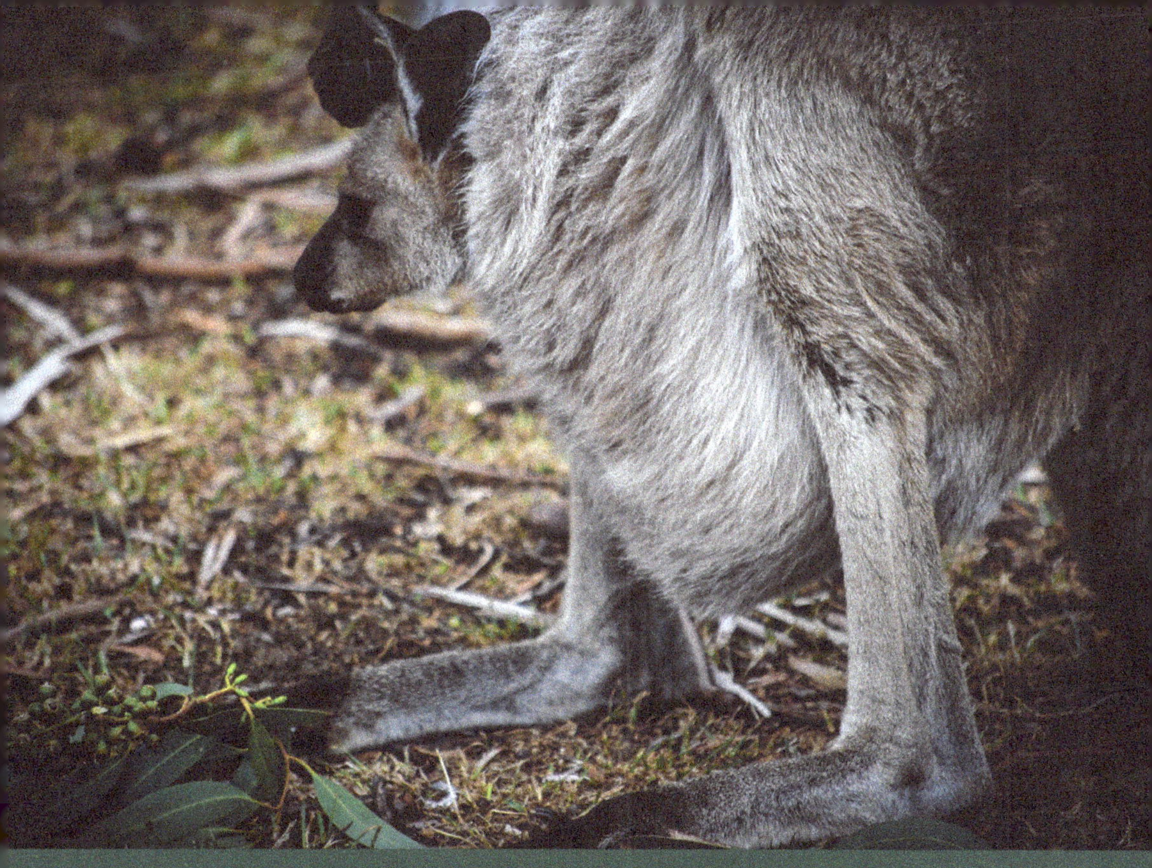

After an hour of adventuring on his own, Joey was happy to return to the safety of home. His mother's unconditional love made him feel brave and confident.

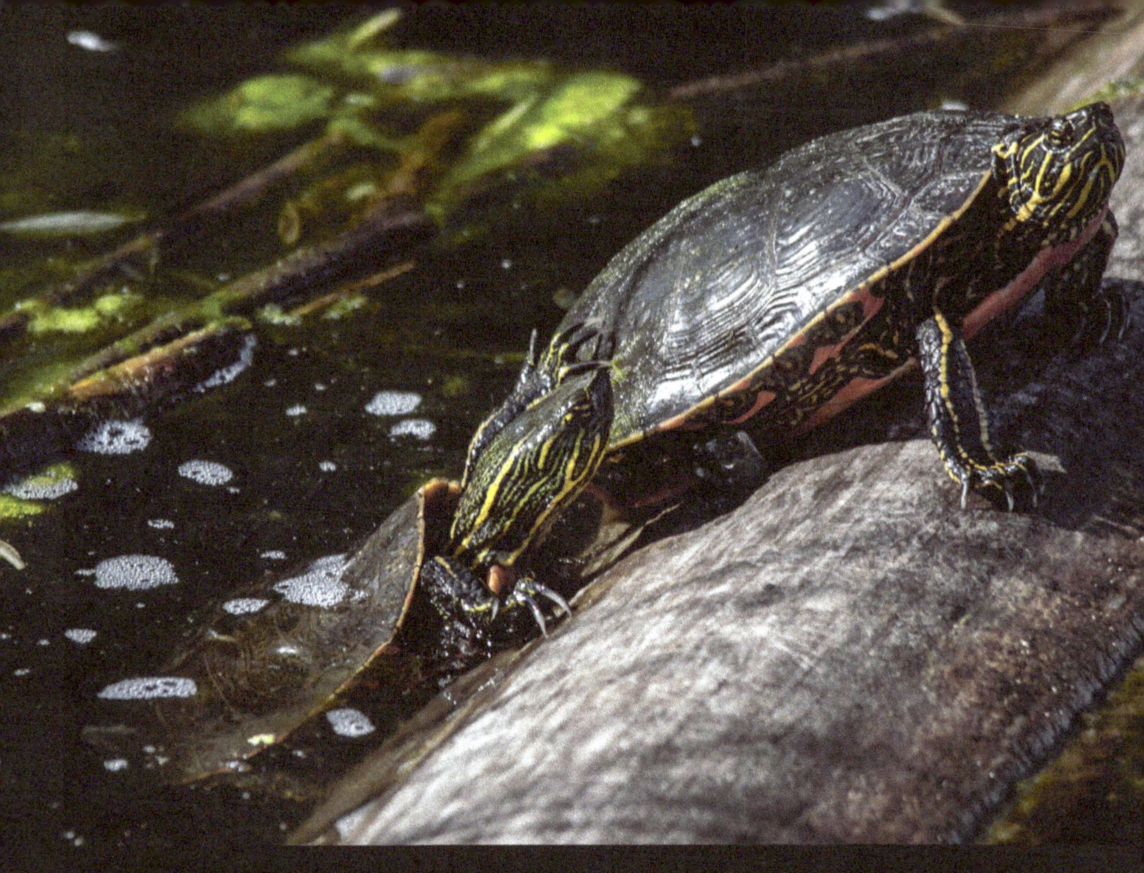

She wished her pal would learn to climb slippery logs on his own and stop using her as a climbing rock. But their conversations, once he finally made it, were worth the minor annoyance.

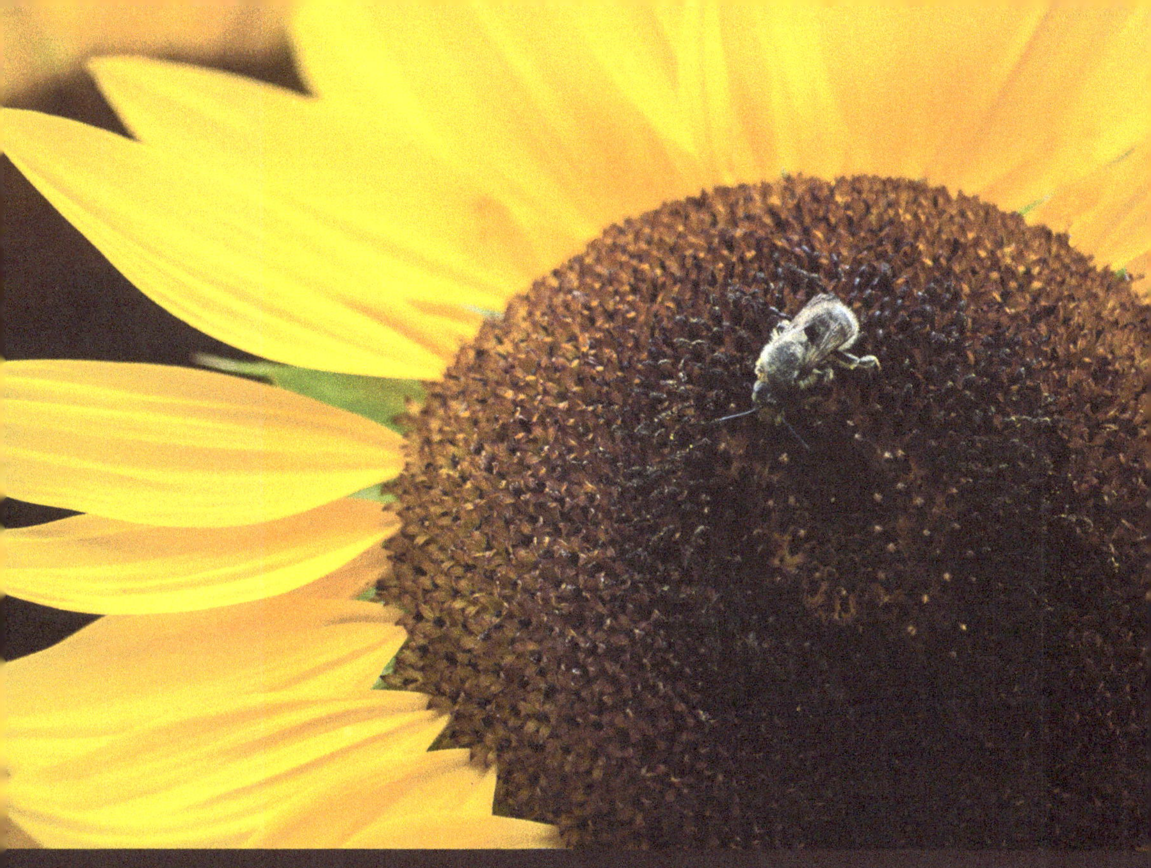

"Oh, Sunflower, I love you so. You are exquisite."
That's what she longed to hear. Instead, all her
insect visitors ever said was, "Yummy! Delicious!
More! More! More!"

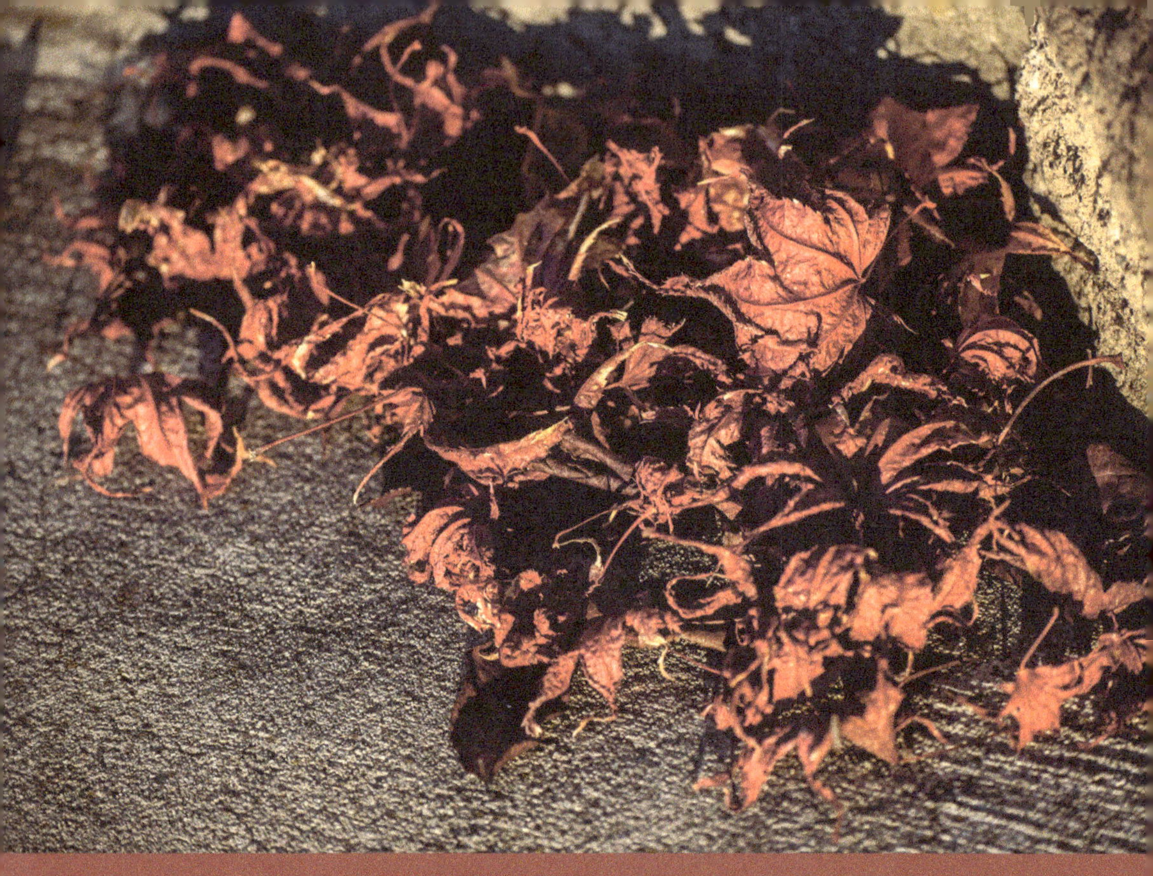

They had danced in the summer winds, shimmered with color as temperatures plunged, twirled gracefully as they let go of their tree. Now it was time to say goodbye. They gathered for a farewell hug.

ABOUT THE AUTHOR

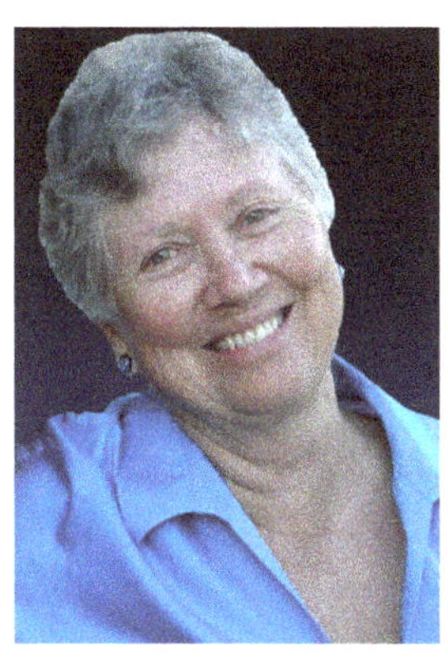

Cathryn Wellner is a writer, photographer and storyteller living in Kelowna, British Columbia, Canada.

Recent books by Cathryn include:
Parts of Me Are Still Amazing
Hope Wins
Feisty Aging
In the Hug of Hills
Millie's Feathered Foster Family
Turkey Baby and the Hungry Hawk
Turkey Baby Finds Her Magic
Cloud Talk

You can find links to these and her other books at cathrynwellner.com. Contact her at cathryn@cathrynwellner.com or 778-478-2760. Her photographs can be found on her Web site, as well as on Facebook and Instagram.

BE A BOOK REVIEW ANGEL

If you enjoyed this book, please post a review on Amazon or Goodreads. Share it with friends and rave about it on social media. You can contact the author at cathryn@cathrynwellner.com.

Authors rely on their readers to help spread the word about books they like. People who review books are special kinds of reader angels. I guarantee when you review this book, or any other book that has given you pleasure in any way, you'll feel those wings poking out your back. Look closely in the mirror, and you might even see a halo.

Credits

Cover fonts: Saltash and BasicSans. Interior font: Bw Surco. Logo font: Ed's Market. Cover background by Pixie Paints Fine Art Textures. (All licensed through DesignCuts.)

Stardust background behind the Introduction is from Sebastian Michaels's amazing Photoshop Artistry course. The heart-shaped hot air balloon is used with permission of the talented foxeysquirrel.

Cover photo of the girl looking up is from Pixabay.com. The book was designed in Photoshop.

Thank you to the amazingly creative people who designed all of the above.

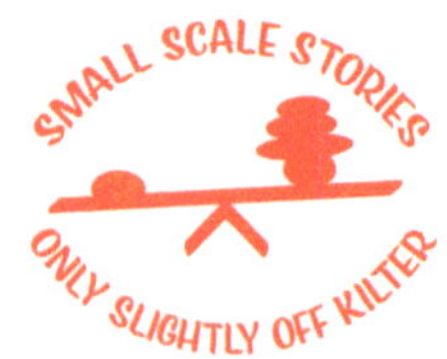

www.ingramcontent.com/pod-product-compliance
Lightning Source LLC
Chambersburg PA
CBHW041050050726
47599CB00018B/2100